PENGUIN BOOKS

ALL EARS

Jill Jarnow has written and illustrated five books on needlework and written four young-adult novels. A founding member of the Long Island Children's Museum, she also serves on the boards of East Woods School in Oyster Bay, New York, and the Ocean Beach Youth Group. She lives in Northport, New York.

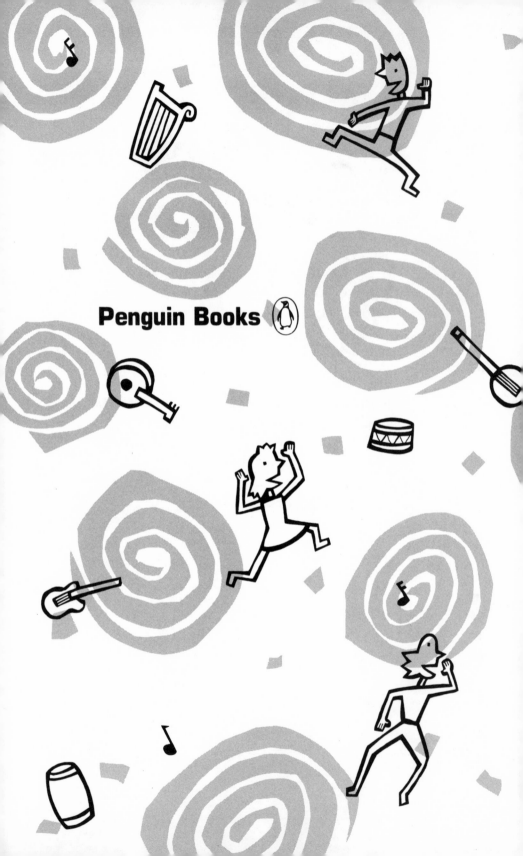

Penguin Books

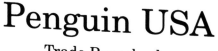

Penguin USA

Trade Paperbacks

With the compliments of
THE AUTHOR

375 Hudson Street
New York, NY 10014

All Ears

How to Choose and Use Recorded Music for Children

Jill Jarnow

PENGUIN BOOKS

Published by the Penguin Group

Viking Penguin, a division of Penguin Books USA Inc.,

375 Hudson Street, New York, New York 10014, U.S.A.

Penguin Books Ltd, 27 Wrights Lane, London W8 5TZ, England

Penguin Books Australia Ltd, Ringwood, Victoria, Australia

Penguin Books Canada Ltd, 2801 John Street, Markham, Ontario, Canada L3R 1B4

Penguin Books (N.Z.) Ltd, 182–190 Wairau Road,

Auckland 10, New Zealand

Penguin Books Ltd, Registered Offices:

Harmondsworth, Middlesex, England

First published in simultaneous hardcover

and paperback editions by Viking Penguin,

a division of Penguin Books USA Inc. 1991

10 9 8 7 6 5 4 3 2 1

LIBRARY OF CONGRESS CATALOGING IN PUBLICATION DATA

Jarnow, Jill.

   All ears : how to choose and use recorded music for children

/ by Jill Jarnow.

      p.   cm.

   Includes bibliographical references and index.

   ISBN 0 14 01.1254 5

   1. Music—Juvenile sound recordings—History and criticism.

I. Title.

MT6.J27A4   1991

780'.83 — dc20   90-7849

Printed in the United States of America

Set in ITC Garamond Light Condensed

Designed by Michael Ian Kaye

Illustrations by Robert Zimmerman

All Ears is dedicated to my family.

To my mother-in-law, Jeannette Jarnow, for listening to ROSENSHONTZ over and over again in the car as we drove through the English countryside with Jesse, then age four. It was above and beyond the call of grandmotherly duty.

To my nephew, Dan Potter, who, in the tradition of Los Angeles trendsetting, introduced us to the music of "Weird Al" Yankovic five years ago.

To my parents, Mel and Lois Stamberg. "Thank you" is hardly enough. My mother led and sometimes dragged my brother and me to radio broadcasts, concerts, and plays when we were children and encouraged us to go on our own when we became young adults. My father did a lot of driving back and forth to New York City in the dark ages of the 1950s and '60s, when Long Island was still sleeping. It was he who missed most of a historic Clancy Brothers / Tommy Makem concert at the 92nd Street Y in 1959 because there was no place to park the car.

To my brother, Peter, who loves to listen as much as I do. I know I can count on him to sing with me every song from every Broadway show we ever saw together. However, I still remember a major disagreement we had in 1959 over who *really* owned the 45-rpm copy of "Sea Cruise." (Of course it was mine.)

To my husband, Al, who has been patient and worked hard to overcome his innate skepticism, allowing me to escort him to selected concerts. He'll never admit it, but I've seen him have a good time.

And most of all, to our son, Jesse, presently age eleven, who, having attended a fair number of concerts and shows and having listened to a myriad of recordings, has developed very definite tastes of his own. That's as it should be—but does it have to be so loud?

I love you all.

Contents

Acknowledgments

All Ears could not have happened without the generosity and support of my family and friends—old and new.

First, of course, I am indebted to the many committed performers, producers, distributors, and publicists who sent me recordings and spent hour upon hour talking to me about music for children and the meaning of life.

Special thanks go to Bill Harley and Debbie Block; Barry Louis Polisar; Mary Miché; Francine Lancaster; Bill Usher; Steve MacArthur; Jill Person; Mark Jaffe; Lieb Ostrow; Anne Ruethling of Chinaberry; Phil Rosenthal; Claudia Rosenthal of Zango; and Dennis and Linda Ronberg.

Thanks to Cliff Fenster and Bob Stanford at Soundtraks in Huntington, New York, for their good-natured willingness to carry music for children.

Thanks to all the families who listened to recordings and reported back to me, especially Randy and Morty Globus; Nicky Colen; Lisa Greene; Richard, Adam, and Amanda Hamburger; Sally Ingraham; Mary Jane Ihasz; Suzanne Garver, Patty, Amanda, and Drew Ingraham; Ilene Maggio; Amy Berkower; Dan, Sarah, and Matthew Weiss; and my cousins Melanie Ress and Ting, Noah, and Eloise Barrow.

Special thanks to P. J. Swift of "Pickleberry Pie" for sharing her vast expertise and well-founded opinions about recordings for families.

Thanks to Paul Butler and his ambitious Imagination Celebration radio concert series at WFDU in Teaneck, New Jersey, which brought so many wonderful performers within an hour's drive.

Thanks to Dr. Robert Abramson, who was so supportive of this project and so generous with his time and insights as we sat under the hot Caribbean sun.

Extra-special thanks to Jamie Deming of Children's Radio Productions for her unique brand of enthusiasm and determination, for driving intrepidly and often to Teaneck, for assembling the up-to-date listing of radio shows for children, and for too much more to mention here.

Thanks to the research librarians at Northport Public Library and to Jane Reiser, librarian at the East Woods School, for whom no request was too obscure.

And thanks to Michael Millman, my editor at Viking Penguin, for his patience and ability to wield the shovel necessary to dig me out from under pounds of paper entitled *All Ears*.

Special note: If I have forgotten to acknowledge my debt to you, please understand. My memory has been enhanced dramatically by a Super Learning listening tape, but it's still not perfect.

Introduction

Human beings have been making, using, and enjoying music in their families for as long as they have been on earth. Why, then, is it suddenly so important to pay attention to our family's musical diet?

As our babies grow into young children, music blaring from the radio and television fills their heads with potent messages. Energized with music, advertisements extol the virtues of eating a Big Mac. Commercial rock music, slick and catchy, glamorizes the glories of life in the fast lane; it's easy for our kids to believe that these are the values on which they should model their lives.

What kind of world is this that our children see as their reality? Are they really failures if they don't wear the right jeans or the right perfume or drive the right car? What happened to feeling good about oneself, to valuing people for who they are and what they can do rather than what they look like or what they own?

The All Ears Alternative

In a move to counteract this cultural evolution, educators, writers, and performers are now directing their creative energies toward producing high-quality music for children and adults to listen to together. While many adults are used to thinking of children's music as condescending, or second best, today's sophisticated recordings offer a wealth of sounds for savvy parents and teachers to enjoy along with the children in their lives. Based on both traditional and contemporary sounds, today's recorded music for children is enhanced by lyrics that are poetic, symbolic, positive, sometimes rude or irreverent, and often just plain fun.

Independent Artists

Many of these wonderful recordings have been intelligently written, performed, and produced by dedicated, talented artists who want to help children and care givers feel their places in the world. While the recordings of a few of these artists are now widely available in chain toy and record stores, the work of hundreds of others, through no fault of their own, remains available only through independent sources.

Cable TV and video producers are starting to pay attention to performers of music for families. You and your children may already have enjoyed seeing Raffi, ROSENSHONTZ, Linda Arnold, Gary Lapow, or Sharon, Lois and Bram on that all-powerful screen at home.

For most recording artists, the secret to survival is to produce their own recordings. In addition, many artists establish hectic performing schedules. By giving hundreds of concerts for children and their parents and teachers, these artists are carving their own special musical niches in people's lives.

The Musical Grapevine

But the best way to learn about what's going on in the world of music for children is through word of mouth. Children and adults are delighted to share their enthusiasm for music they like.

Eight years ago I stood in the children's room of the Northport Public Library flipping through a stack of records, looking for something new and exciting to listen to with my three-year-old son, Jesse. Xander Marro, then six, had come up next to me and was waiting for her turn to go through the pile. "That one is really great," she volunteered as I turned up an album by ROSENSHONTZ, a group unfamiliar to me. On Xander's recommendation, I took it to the circulation desk and checked it out.

And she was right. ROSENSHONTZ's *Tickles You!* became an instant family favorite. We listened to it constantly. Jesse's grandmother Jeannette, who heard it many times when we vacationed together over the summer, came to like the music so much that she took the train out to Long Island to see ROSENSHONTZ give a family concert.

Several years later, when I asked Xander how she had learned about ROSEN-SHONTZ in the first place, she told me that her uncle from Vermont, ROSEN-SHONTZ's home state, had sent her an album for her birthday. Thank you, Uncle Albert!

The All Ears Mission

Over the last nine years I have listened to scores of new recordings as they became available, enjoying the evolution of "kids' music." With the passage of time, I have come to realize that what we once so derogatorily labeled "kids' music" is really an intelligent, important genre that we should now identify as "family music." It's music that families can enjoy listening to together.

As a labor of love, I have spent countless hours going to concerts, listening to the radio, and sorting through the wealth of musical recordings as they became available, amassing listings of many important albums that might otherwise be missed. In writing descriptions of the musical style and thematic content of each album and giving it a carefully considered age-appeal rating, my goal is to help parents, care givers, teachers, and librarians make selections that will entertain, excite, comfort, and educate them together with the children they love.

What Is Family Listening?

Family listening is an activity—high on the list of "quality time" activities—in which children and their care givers enjoy listening together to the same recording. They can listen to recordings in the kitchen, in the bedroom, or in the car. They can listen on a rainy afternoon, just before dinner, or at any time that feels right to them. While music teachers can continue to use listening to enhance their students' understanding of music, other educators can enrich classroom lessons in science, history, math, and language arts with today's crop of new recordings.

Power Versus Empowerment

Today's revolutionary new music often addresses issues that help children understand themselves and decipher the world they live in. While contemporary pop music wields its awesome power over us, contemporary music for family listening gives us the raw materials of personal empowerment, offering listeners important messages about human values and experiences. Families who listen together, sing along together, laugh together, and talk together become families who grow strong together.

Your mission is to find recordings that everyone in the family will love. It's not a hard job. The music is out there waiting for you.

Why Good Listening Makes Good Sense

Throughout history, music has been used by people of every culture to share messages of inspiration about religion and state, to pass on personal or public history, to inspire, to glorify, to express love, anger, despair, and hope, to amuse, to relax, and to educate. Nurturing parents use musical messages to comfort, bond with, and communicate with their infants. Babies use music to explore and develop their listening and speaking skills. Children use music to gather information as well as to sort out their feelings, ideas, and experiences.

The Mysterious Power of Music

In its simplest definition, music is sound organized to move through time and space. But what is the difference between the sound of feet clicking down the street and the sound of an African drum call? Both are capable of eliciting an emotional response, and both have a rhythm. Yet there is one important distinction: the sounds of the drum are thoughtfully organized; the sounds of the feet clicking are not.

Music has the ability to go beyond words to stimulate the feelings and emotions of listeners through rhythm, tempo, melody, harmony, pitch, and repetition. Musicians combine these elements into patterns of movements and gestures that convey feelings, pictures, ideas, and symbols.

Although many people have theories about how music communicates, not everyone agrees about exactly how emotional cues are transmitted. Educators can define and teach the mechanics of the composing and performing processes; yet the experiences of the composer and the performer, as well as the experience of the listener, remain a mystery.

The Importance of Early Music Interactions

Music is an aural, kinesthetic, and mental phenomenon which depends upon our ears for processing. While a newborn's hearing is probably as acute at birth as it is ever likely to be, and most babies hear well enough to process musical sounds, as they grow, so develops their ability to focus on sounds. Infancy and early-childhood experts now concur that the parents can enhance the development of their children's communication and perception skills through early musical interaction.

When you hum, chant, and croon to your newborn during your daily routines together, you are instinctively establishing special listening times. While you may consider this interaction to be too natural and mundane to deserve comment, you may not realize why these exchanges are so valuable. In addition to offering essential nurturing, the babbling sounds and rhythms that you exchange with your baby represent the first steps he or she takes toward communicating through speech.

Learning to speak is a process that is activated when your baby hears your conversations. According to childhood educator, lecturer, and amateur musician John Holt, a child learns to speak "by trying many thousands of times to make sounds, syllables and words; by comparing his own sounds to the sounds made by people around him; and by gradually bringing his own sounds closer to the others; above all, by being willing to do things wrong even while trying his best to do them right." Babies who are raised in understaffed foundling hospitals, he has observed, while able to cry, grow up to be almost mute.

Listening Enrichment for Your Baby

Zoltán Kodály, the composer and childhood specialist, contended that not only do babies and young children enjoy hearing music from their parents, but frequent and quality listening with a primary care giver enhances children's ability to concentrate. Infants who are encouraged to concentrate through music listening, he observed, are better able to discriminate important patterns of sound that result in enriched language development, reading ability, and coordination. Recognizing the same phenomenon, music educator Émile Jaques-Dalcroze reasoned that it is the control of balance and body movements along with the use of the senses that prepares children to develop the skills of attention and concentration that they need to thrive in school. When children feel comfortable following their senses, their muscles are relaxed yet alert, and all channels are open to observe, concentrate, and learn.

In light of these observations, music educator John M. Feierabend, an exponent of the Kodály theory of music education, has made an eye-opening comment about our contemporary style of parenting. "Playpens, mechanical swings and television have replaced all-important musical dialogues between parent and child," he tells us. "Today, parents are unfamiliar with the wealth of musical activities that have served many generations. Yet, ask grandparents to recommend a song or game they enjoyed with their children, and you will witness the reconstruction of a loving, human interaction that has no equal!"

Child-development experts have also discovered that the quality and quantity of what infants and toddlers absorb before the age of three is related directly to their later language development. Whether or not the child understands what she hears is unimportant. She needs merely to absorb it. Unconscious listening, it seems, is a necessary first step toward good conscious listening.

For parents, it's reassuring to know that although there is no way to make formal measurements, the seemingly ordinary activities and conversations we have with our babies, even when these things don't seem very "musical," combine with the music we choose to play in our homes to enhance the development of our children's intellectual and physical skills.

Simple Sounds That Help Your Baby Grow

In addition to singing for your baby at every opportunity, play a music box for her before nap time. As your baby becomes a toddler, provide simple musical instruments such as a drum or a wood block that she can play to discover where sounds come from.

Help your toddler grow into a child who listens to music with enthusiasm by encouraging her to play at making simple sounds. Children must learn through experience that musical sounds come from a variety of people and instruments singing and playing in a variety of ways before they can understand and enjoy groups of people making music together.

If you are a musician, your children will love hearing you play simple melodies for them. Even if you consider yourself merely a dabbling musician, dabble within earshot of your young children. Or in the absence of musical skills, seek out musical friends and ask them to perform for your family. Assure reluctant musicians embarrassed that they are "rusty" that simple tunes are the order of the day and that young listeners are not interested in making value judgments about the quality of the performance. Instead, seeing and hearing music produced from a musical instrument is an experience that a young child will long cherish.

The Importance of Music for Young Children

Early-childhood educator and researcher Dorothy McDonald has observed that preschool children create and explore music with more energy and spontaneity than any other age group. Many preschoolers, whether at rest or at play, self-confidently accompany their activities with a steady stream of personal rhythms, tunes, and words.

But while children so easily embrace music in their early years, McDonald is dismayed to find that some of today's educators take a casual attitude toward the musical experiences of preschool students. Music is generally considered to be a pleasant yet isolated and expendable component of the classroom experience. McDonald advises teachers to go beyond reserving music experiences solely for "music time," since this is not the way children naturally use it. She urges professionals instead to incorporate interactive listening, rhythm, and movement games into many aspects of daily classroom life.

To be most effective in the school setting, the learning process must be nurtured at home. Parents who understand that their children grow and develop in ways that are not immediately visible can, in good faith, continue to seek out enjoyable, age-appropriate musical experiences for their families.

By singing and playing informal rhythm and music games with their preschool and early-elementary-age children, parents can prepare them for important new levels of learning. By providing enjoyable, age-appropriate recordings to listen to together, parents can encourage their children to experiment with melody, rhythms, patterns of sounds and words. As they listen to music, preschoolers amass tools that become important to them when they are developmentally ready to learn. Combined with drawing, painting, and looking at the words and pictures in books, music listening helps children achieve eye movement in rhythmically organized patterns that facilitate reading skills.

How Music for Elementary-Age Children Enhances Reading, Writing, Understanding, Thinking, and Remembering

Music activities enhance the continuous and unconscious process of learning for all elementary-age students. Researchers tell us that many of children's manifest abilities come from years of unconscious development. In 1987, *Gifted Child Monthly* encapsulated a report from the Roeper Review that concluded that investigation in a variety of disciplines, including neurology, education, psychology, and linguistics, revealed evidence that early music training can stimulate superior intellectual development.

By integrating music and other forms of art into their classroom subjects, teachers raise the interest level of their students while creating experiences that have lasting meaning for them. For many students, having music blended into curriculum topics—language arts, math, history, science—enables them to develop academic skills that might otherwise remain elusive.

Relating music activities to classroom subjects enhances the depth of students' understanding, motivation, discipline, and memory. Listening, responding to, and performing music and other forms of artistic exploration in a context meaningful to them stimulates students' imaginations, encourages them to develop alternate ways of thinking, and sharpens their problem-solving skills.

The College Board, an organization that focuses on academic achievement, emphasizes in its handbook the need for children to be active in the arts at every level of their school careers. As school districts continue to trim their budgets by cutting back on arts programs, concerned parents and teachers in cooperation with elementary and secondary-school policymakers will want to find ways to keep children involved in the arts.

Music Listening Beyond the Classroom

Because academic accomplishment and positive family interaction are intertwined, parents will want to bring music listening into their homes as a frequent family activity. In addition to enhancing classroom skills, family listening promotes self-esteem through family peace and understanding. In our video-oriented, pressure-cooker world, family listening is a valuable tool for establishing both meaningful communication and a joyful structure to help your family relax together.

Your Child's Gifts

All Ears is based on the premise that all children are born with their own inherent gifts, which will be enhanced and amplified by listening and interacting with music and people. Scientists and educators are beginning to realize that early, positive musical experiences are uniquely important to all children because they provide them with valuable building blocks for developing physical coordination, timing, memory, and visual, aural, and linguistic skills. In a report in *Gifted Child Monthly,* researcher Emily P. Cary concluded that "the home enriched by music is more likely to produce gifted children than the unmusical home."

But is your child *musically* gifted? While nearly everyone has the ability to enjoy listening and even performing, some people are simply more musical than others. Your child may or may not be musically gifted. The important question to ask is: Is your child musically *active*? If you see that your young child takes an unusual pleasure in the musical activities you share at home and those that she experiences in early preschool classes, I urge you to provide her with the opportunity to develop her interest by studying an appropriate, structured method of music education.

Music Education for Children

In addition to nurturing your child's natural love of music at home through playful, improvised listening, singing, and rhythm and movement games, you may want to provide formal music education. Many preschool programs include informal musical experiences within their curriculum, but these may be inadequate for stimulating the musically active child. Whether or not you suspect that you are raising the next Van Cliburn, if your child shows particular joy in his musical interactions (and many children do), you will be doing him a big favor by providing a sound, structured method of music education that is suitable to his age, temperament, interests, and personal preference.

There are four important methods of teaching music to children: Jaques-Dalcroze, Kodály, Orff, and Comprehensive Musicianship. Although each approach is distinctly different in philosophy, tools, and technique, there is some overlap in ideology, and the goals and methods of each have been influenced by the "discover everything" principles of educator Johann Pestalozzi (1747–1827), the first person to attempt to link the educational process to the natural development of the child.

Émile Jaques-Dalcroze

Devised by Swiss educator Émile Jaques-Dalcroze in the 1890s, Eurythmics, or rythmics, is based on the concept that music and movement are inseparable and that the body is a natural instrument for the study of rhythm. Dalcroze has said that "any musical idea may be transformed into movement . . . [and] any body movement may be transformed into its musical counterpart." Musical symbols and instrumental improvisation are added after listening and physical movement experiences ease the way to understanding. Dalcroze students "become" the music as a prelude to further studies in reading, writing, and improvising music.

Orff

The Orff music education program, developed by German-born composer Carl Orff (1895–1982), is based on the idea that feeling comes before understanding. Emphasizing the excitement of making music, Orff specialists encourage children to experiment with speech, chants, and rhythms. The Orff method uses children's rhymes and proverbs as a basis for teaching rhythm, phrasing, and musical expression. Orff students use specially developed instruments for improvisation.

Kodály

The Kodály method of music education, based primarily on singing, was developed in Hungary in the 1940s and '50s by composer Zoltán Kodály (1882–1967). Preschool children experience rhythm by enacting the words of nursery songs: they "row the boat," "rock the baby," and play traditional children's games. Older children learn musical vocabulary and reading through folk songs. Kodály developed a system of hand signals to help a child "see" the notes of the scale that they hear. Musical skills are developed through a step-by-step curriculum, so that by their teen years children can sight-read and sight-sing.

Comprehensive Musicianship

Comprehensive Musicianship was formalized in 1965 as an outgrowth of the Young Composers Project and the Contemporary Music Project for Creativity in Music Education. CM students are encouraged to become composers, listeners, and performers through discovery and experimentation with sounds and sound sources and through knowledge of music of all styles, periods, and cultures.

Introducing the Great Family-Listening Habit

We live in a luxurious world of constant music. While we listen to music by choice when we attend concerts, ballets, and operas, we are enveloped by music whenever we turn on the radio or television, attend movies, or walk through the supermarket.

We can hear—but how well do we *listen*? The barrage of sounds and sights that fills our lives can overwhelm and undermine the development of our children's abilities to listen, concentrate, communicate, and think. By helping our children to sort and select, we can encourage them to turn from passive "absorbers" to active "listeners." We can ensure that they develop precious skills that they might otherwise lose.

While hearing is a purely physical sensation, listening involves analyzing the details and meanings of patterns of sound. It is an active process through which the listener must concentrate, using many of his senses, in order to understand what's going on. To listen is to make a conscious effort to make sense out of what one hears. How well one listens affects how well one is able to learn, grow, and interact with the world. While school curricula address the teaching of more tangible topics, listening skills are best nurtured and developed in a family setting.

What Is Family Listening?

"Family," once simply defined as a father, a mother, and their children, must now be redefined as a child or group of children and their primary care giver or care givers. The care giver is the adult who spends the most time with a child and has the greatest opportunity to enhance the child's emotional and intellectual development.

Family listening is an activity during which a child and an adult focus their attention on positive, high-quality music that is geared both to the ears, bodies, feelings, and mind of the growing child as well as to the supportive, evolving family. Sometimes a child will listen to the music alone, sometimes the adult will listen alone; but ultimately the child and adult spend time listening and sharing family-listening recordings together.

For the first time ever, a wide range of recordings are available to match the developmental needs and interests of infants, toddlers, preschoolers, and elementary-age children. In addition to being entertaining, many of these recordings, when used sensitively by an adult, can stimulate, educate, and reassure listeners of all ages.

Developing Good Habits

In this era of people struggling to break destructive addictions like drug abuse, smoking, overeating, or watching too much TV, it's refreshing to know that we can actually bring new and constructive habits into our lives. The family-listening habit is a positive activity that rarely gets mentioned, and yet it can do so much for everyone's well-being.

While some adults fall easily into the family-listening habit, perhaps without realizing just how beneficial it is, others who feel that they are simply "unmusical" have to be coerced or prodded into it by a loving friend or relative or even by their children. Some adults shy away from "kids' music" because they haven't allowed themselves to appreciate its value. But no matter how families come to it, listening to music together adds to the quality of family life like nothing else. Family listening promotes thinking and language development, the ability to concentrate, coordinate, and imagine. Music for family listening accentuates positive values, ideas, and behavior, opens paths of communication between people and generations, and becomes a delightful activity that everyone in the family can enjoy together.

Family Listening and the Skeptical Adult

For many adults with established listening tastes of their own, the first response is one of revulsion. Some adults, having had bad experiences with "kids' music," are convinced that it all must be saccharine, condescending, or mindless even as they overlook the limitations of popular adult music, which often dwells simplistically on romantic love and the loss of personal power.

But even the most sophisticated music connoisseurs can discover their attitude shifting once they begin to experience the world as parents. Adults, especially those who are determined to be "active" (or "quality") parents, are often astonished when they grow to enjoy "kids' music" as much as their children do. Movie critic Janet Maslin of *The New York Times* acknowledged the evolution in her own attitudes: "Before my son was born . . . someone gave us a tape of Raffi singing folk songs for children and we listened for only a few minutes before deciding our friends had taken leave of their senses. These days, Raffi might as well be Mick Jagger."

Musical Styles of Family Listening: Something for Everyone

In recognition of the need for diversity, the field of music for family listening has grown within the last five years to encompass a myriad of musical styles and sounds. Folk, rock, jazz, Broadway, disco, pop, and cross-cultural sounds are all represented on recordings for family listening. Some performers, like Kevin Roth and Raffi, are warm and gentle; others, like Barry Louis Polisar and Peter Alsop, are outrageous and blunt. Jon Crosse plays lullabies in a jazz idiom, while Francine Lancaster sings nursery rhymes in a classical style. Phil Rosenthal records traditional bluegrass music for kids, while Tickle Tune Typhoon has an eclectic, full sound reminiscent of Stephen Sondheim.

In Defense of the Preachy

Music for family listening advocates positive values, our right to be individuals, and empowerment for all people, especially children. Family-listening recordings reassure and inspire listeners by artfully sharing common experiences through music and lyrics.

If some of the recordings recommended for family listening sound "preachy" to you (and I've heard that complaint from a few adults), it's because human beings have proven that these techniques are an effective way to share ideas. Rap has an especially strong presence in pop music right now; but the most powerful institutions of civilization long have used narrative singing and repetition to disseminate their messages. We acknowledge and welcome these techniques when they come to us at our houses of worship, and yet we often try to ignore and deny the same methods when they come at us from TV and radio. We are so acclimated to hearing commercial pop music that many of us cannot see beyond song lyrics focused on the pain and glory of love—a tradition built by the music industry primarily for its commercial value. For the well-being of our children, let's acknowledge that there are other human experiences to sing about, other ways to think and act, other values to glorify.

The Impact of Music

Although we rarely stop to acknowledge it, music wields awesome power in our lives. We find ourselves focused on the most unexpected images and products when they are presented to us with upbeat musical accompaniments. The emotional impact of movies, television shows, and commercials is heightened by state-of-the-art theme songs, background music, and jingles. While it's no accident that our children can sing every word in the latest McDonald's commercial before they are old enough to go to kindergarten, it is more than a little frightening. Television advertising, enhanced by music, tells our children they must wear the right clothes and play with the right toys; to be somebody, they must eat and drink specific name-brand foods at specific places. Commercial television has become a window to the world through which our children learn, with the help of skillfully scored music, that to be grown up is to be glamorous, sheeplike consumers living in a world punctuated by violence.

At the same time, when our children listen to the newest hard rock on the radio, they hear music that is often violent and racist. Not much better, soft-sounding adult contemporary rock and even the golden oldies of the fifties and sixties bombard them with messages that advocate narrow values and offer as gospel stereotyped patterns for behavior and role modeling. Over and over again our children hear "I'm nothing without you." To be somebody you must be in love, and to be in love means to be a slave. In the world of pop and country music, it's the only way to know who you are.

Messages are couched in catchy, rhythmic music that people listen to over and over again. We listened to it as children, and many of us still do. It seems innocuous until we stop to think about the long-range effects of the messages. Instead of endorsing the value of developing inner strength, skills, and individual styles of thinking, much of pop music offers rigid, impossible models for living our lives. Many adults find it painful and overwhelming when they finally discover that there's a real world behind all the music, glitz, and hype.

As the first generation to have been exposed to this musical media brainwashing generated by commercial television, radio, and movies, we are the first group to experience its effects. As loving and active parents, let's prevent our children from being overly impressed by those glamorous yet misleading messages. Instead, let's seek out commercial and independently produced music that will encourage our children to appreciate the value of diversity. Let's help our children to set their own realistic and worthwhile priorities the first time around!

How Parents Can Cope with the Commercial Media

What exactly does "commercial media" mean? It means programming, advertising, and product offerings that exist with little regard for social responsibility, often for the benefit of the commercial establishment.

Not all that happens on the commercial media is bad or without value. Thoughtful programming does exist on our commercial airwaves; there is responsible advertising for worthwhile products and services. But media content is unpredictable. When it's good, it can be excellent; but when it's bad, it can be lethal. You, as the guardian of the young and trusting consumers in your household, must look critically at what your kids are seeing and hearing. We may dismiss most network programming as noneducational; but the fact is that our kids are learning *too* much from it.

Children are naturally driven to find their place in the world. When they watch too much irresponsible television or listen to too much commercial radio, *it* becomes their world. While our children are presented with pictures of unattainable physical beauty and wealth and oversimplified interpersonal relationships, they are shown very little of the struggles and growth that give value to human life.

Worst of all, while they watch television our children become numb to their own emotions and ideas. Left unchecked, the commercial media become your child's most influential—and most destructive—teachers.

When it comes to playing adult-oriented music, you will, of course, follow your own heart. But if you stop and listen to the words of your favorite songs and realize that your children are remarkably perceptive listeners, I think you will find it alarming when your five-year-old sings "Like a Virgin" or "(I Can't Get No) Satisfaction." Listen to how pop music advocates narrow, one-dimensional behavior and attitudes. Children absorb this information and use it to guide their judgments as they mature. Reevaluate serving them a steady diet of commercial music. Instead, search through *All Ears* for satisfying musical supplements that you can enjoy together.

Responsible Viewing and Listening

Unless you live on a mountaintop without electricity, you cannot shield your children completely from commercial media. Whether we like it or not, commercial programming is the culture of our day.

To deny your children total access to commercial TV, radio, and the movies is to turn it into forbidden fruit, and to label anything forbidden is to give it more importance than it deserves. On the other hand, to let your children watch and listen to anything and everything that appeals to them for as long as they like can have some appalling results. Instead, understand the long-term effects that commercial television and radio will have on your children and find a realistic middle ground. Find out what quality programming has been produced for children. And pay close attention to age-appropriate ratings—your six-year-old and your fourteen-year-old are not ready to process the same information. By providing stimulating alternatives, you can make sure that the commercial media are a minor aspect of your children's lives. To succeed will take thoughtful and active parenting, but your kids are worth it.

The Benefits of Family Listening

Family listening reduces family hassling.

The recordings listed in *All Ears* range from the upbeat and humorous to the gentle and soothing. If you make your selections with sensitivity, you can provide music to defuse potential family conflicts by encouraging family members to relax and refocus. Riding in the car (either to the grocery store or during a family vacation), being stuck indoors in bad weather or because the outdoors is otherwise inaccessible, or having to grin and bear your way through household chores are all improved when accompanied by thoughtfully chosen music.

The object of family listening is to use music as a conduit to share common experiences. Rather than arguing whose turn it is, who is sitting in whose spot, or who ate the last cookie, you can listen and laugh at the same jokes, think quietly about the same engrossing story, wait to hear a favorite song or line or tune, tap or clap to the rhythm or all sing along. Hassles are minimized, because everybody is concentrating on the music.

Family listening is for all ages.

Everyone, no matter what his age or talent, can listen at his own level. With a little careful investigating, you will be able to find recordings that can be enjoyed by siblings of assorted ages as well as by parents and grandparents.

Family listening is nonjudgmental.

Singing together as a group is more constructive than focusing on individual skills or lack of skills. Instead, open the door for everyone to participate by reaffirming everyone's right to participate at his or her own level. No one is too young or too untalented to participate. Everyone has a place.

While the ability to carry a tune can be an area for passing judgment among family members, parents will want to establish early the tone for acceptance. Singing together is more fun and valuable as an activity than the product you create. Discourage negative judgments from group members—it's not necessary to sound like the Mormon Tabernacle Choir.

Family listening enhances imagination.

Imagination is an important asset of humanity. As an antidote to an overdose of television watching, family listening stimulates the regeneration of children's ability to think abstractly. Whether focused on the radio or tuned in to a recording, children must exercise their minds using a variety of senses to construct imaginary pictures suggested by the music and words they hear.

Family listening helps families grow together by promoting positive human values and self-esteem.

Family listening can help everyone in the family become aware of contemporary issues of family and school and the world we live in by encouraging people of all ages, abilities, and backgrounds to understand and appreciate each other. By taking the time to talk with your family about the words of a song, you will initiate valuable dialogue. Especially when our children get such strong messages from mass media about the acceptability of violent, self-destructive behavior, it is to every child's advantage to understand what the words *really* mean.

But even if you are not inclined to turn listening into a rap session, by listening repeatedly to the kind of music listed in *All Ears* your child will be exposed to positive ideas. She will learn "I want to be somebody that somebody like me could like" (Malvina Reynolds) in a way similar to how she learned that "Coke is It."

How to Develop the Great Family-Listening Habit

Making Great "Music" Together

You have probably already caught yourself improvising rhythmic tunes while you splash water on your baby in the bathtub or wheel her down the street. You may even have discovered how seemingly mindless ditties that emerge from your mouth do just the trick at diaper-changing time, distracting your baby from the indignity of having her bottom wiped.

Though you know you'll never sound like Beverly Sills or Plácido Domingo, instinctively it feels right to make these sounds for your infant. And it is. Using a tradition as old as parenthood, with simple songs and improvised chants you are easing difficult moments and bringing you and your baby closer together.

If ever a moment of self-consciousness has crept into your performance as you set about to sing your baby to sleep with a lullaby, be assured that even the most unmusical of parents sound magnificent to their babies. Infants are comforted and nurtured by the natural rhythmic sounds of their care givers. Right from the beginning, your baby will understand and grow from your message of comfort.

As your baby grows into a toddler, a preschooler, and beyond, continue to weave your own music into the time you share together. Whether you are doing chores together, like making beds or unpacking grocery bags, or walking down the street, invent impromptu chants, rhymes, or song fragments to accompany your activity.

The Value of Musical Improvisation

Just as your young child will benefit from your ongoing musical improvisations, as she grows she will benefit from her own musical experiments. Don't assume that once your child has reached her early elementary years, her only worthwhile listening experiences come from hearing the formally organized sounds of music being performed either on a recording or in person. Instead, encourage her to continue experimenting with sounds and rhythms of her own creation. Whether children sing or chant their own tunes and songs, play with percussion, strings, or keyboard instruments, experimentation is the key to confidence, pleasure, and growth.

Singing and Dancing Along

Encourage your child to respond to the music he hears by singing, clapping, moving, or dancing. And be sure he hears a variety of rhythms. High-energy, cheerful music is appealing and energizing and is usually communicated through even-tempoed rhythms. But hearing syncopated or contemplative music will give your child additional opportunities to experiment and learn through movement.

Some children move to music instinctively, without self-consciousness or provocation. Others come to enjoy it if they see people around them having a good time. Jamie Deming, creator of the children's radio show "Kids Alive," dances around the kitchen with her children, Peter, age six, and Julia, age four. Visiting playmates at first eye them skeptically, Jamie reports. But when they finally realize that dancing in the kitchen is de rigueur in the Deming household, they are delighted to join in.

Listening to Music Together

As your infant matures, so will grow his ability to enjoy and benefit from music listening. Because everyone develops at a different rate and with different personal preferences, it is often misleading and unsettling to read a generalized overview of stages of development. Be assured that your child will not move into each category listed below on the dot of his birthday.

On the other hand, the following stages, observed by music educators and developmental specialists, will help you understand the major periods that young listeners pass through. By being aware of each plateau you will be better able to choose recordings that you and your family can enjoy together.

Since your child's taste and developmental readiness will be individual, you will succeed in finding what she likes and when she likes it only by experimenting. Built on knowledge and respect, your sensitivity will go a long way toward creating positive and meaningful listening experiences for your family.

Developmental Stages of Listening and Interacting

Newborn

Having spent the previous nine months next to human metronomes, their mothers' hearts, it is no surprise that newborns like to hear rhythmic, soothing sounds while being gently rocked and patted. Parents' instinctive crooning goes a long way toward offering comfort and security to babies. Both parent and baby benefit from listening to lullaby music and gentle musical classics, because the comforting sounds help both listeners focus on relaxing.

As infants near three months, they may become increasingly sensitive to sudden, jarring sounds such as sirens, alarms, and church bells. However, they are also able to appreciate and be calmed by gentle, pretty sounds.

Babies are increasingly fascinated with rich, simple sounds such as a spoon tapping on a glass of water or the pluck of a guitar string. Some babies show interest in more upbeat sounds, responding to popular music on the radio and the music of television commercials.

Being bounced on a parent's lap or knee will become a favorite activity for babies around this age. This is the time for parents to begin sharing their favorite activity chants.

Babies become fascinated with their ability to make noises. They may repeatedly hit, bang, or squeeze rattles, blocks, and other noisemaking toys. Musical mobiles are often big hits with infants—although parents must be sure to hang them well out of reach.

1–2 Years

As infants become toddlers, they are delighted by their emerging ability to coordinate their large body movements to rhythms. Increasingly aware of sounds such as bells, whistles, and clocks, one-year-olds like to identify simple noises such as the buzz of the bee, the meow of the cat, the moo of the cow.

Between one and two, children are pleased to be able to identify their body parts. For activities that enhance these interests, parents should look toward recordings that include simple activities like clapping and finger play.

2–3 Years

At around two years old, children can begin to sing phrases of a familiar song, although often not on pitch. They are fascinated by sounds in general and are delighted with repeated listening, speaking, and singing.

Two-year-olds respond to music rhythmically by bouncing, swaying, swinging their arms, nodding their heads, or tapping their feet. They also enjoy using rhythmical equipment such as swings and rocking chairs, which may inspire them to sing spontaneously. They like to hold another person's hand or grasp an object while walking or dancing to music.

At two and a half, children may know all or parts of several songs. While they may sing spontaneously, they may become unaccountably shy when asked to do it with or for others. At the same time, many children at this age enjoy running, galloping, and swinging to music in a group situation.

Children are capable of becoming much more involved with music at around this age, and show a preference for tunes with marked rhythm. They now enjoy hearing favorites repeatedly much in the way that they enjoy playing with close friends.

3–4 Years

By age three, children can recognize several melodies and sing several simple songs all the way through, though usually not on pitch. They will join group singing with less inhibition.

Three-year-olds can run, jump, and walk, bounce, stomp, and clap in fairly good time to music. Because they are increasingly able to refine their movements, they now enjoy experimenting with a variety of rhythms. Most preschoolers enjoy group activities, and a shy child may join in when invited by a peer.

Children between three and four also enjoy experimenting with music making. They are delighted with simple explanations about songs and instruments. Children now begin to show individual differences in their interest in and ability to listen to music.

By age four, children are better able to control their voices and to approximate correct pitch and rhythm. While only a few can sing an entire song in tune, most children enjoy group singing and enjoy taking turns singing alone.

Four-year-olds enjoy identifying melodies. They show increased pleasure in interpreting rhythms through movement. They can play simple singing games and are particularly interested in songs that dramatize. They create their own songs during play and often use them to tease others.

4–5 Years

Four-year-olds love hearing and singing silly songs. They enjoy games that involve moving to the music, such as "The Hokey Pokey" and "Skip to My Lou." In addition, they thrive on making rhythms and using rhythm instruments to accompany themselves.

Five-year-olds enjoy call-and-response songs. They can repeat simple rhythms by clapping. Not all children can duplicate all simple rhythms, however. Memory and perception of rhythm evolves from personal preference and may reflect rhythmic patterns that they have experienced in daily life. Many children like to keep a beat with their bodies as well as with rhythm instruments.

Many five-year-olds love to experiment with tunes and sounds, making up their own songs—often, the sillier the better.

6–9 Years

Between ages six and eight, children's tonal ability develops rapidly. At around age seven they are able to discern levels of sound. While younger listeners are easily confused and distracted by sounds that are secondary to a simple melody and words, early-elementary-age children can begin to understand that voices and instruments have distinct characteristics in their sounds.

Most elementary-age children can sing a song in its entirety and can remember the melody despite changes in tempo, key, or style of accompaniment. Some youngsters have a sense of melody so well developed that they are capable of holding a tune when singing a round against equally strong voices. Since a child's vocal range may now be expanding significantly, this is an advantageous time to encourage children to listen and sing.

At approximately age seven children enter a stage of development identified by Jean Piaget as the concrete operations period. Music educators feel that it is during this time that, as Edwin Gordon observed in *The Psychology of Music Teaching,* "basic concepts of tonality and rhythm mature and listening perception begins. These three musical aspects are considered to be the core of musical aptitude. The development of these skills during this period may explain why musical aptitude becomes basically set around age nine."

10: The Age of Yuck

According to music-education researcher Steven K. Hedden, children's musical tastes become set at around age ten, at which point parents find it much harder to have a substantial impact on the listening preferences of their children. If only our kids would wait that long! You probably will discover that your children begin to exert their musical opinions earlier.

I have unscientifically dubbed this period of development "the Age of Yuck." It came to our house much too soon, when neither my husband nor I was ready. One day Jesse was happily listening to ROSENSHONTZ, and the next day he was on to the Beatles and the Beach Boys. All new advances I made to introduce him to anything other than "real" rock 'n' roll was repulsed by a loud and meaningful "yuck." Startled, I was thrown off balance for a while, until I discovered that there was one last layer of offerings for young listeners that we could share together.

The Age of Yuck may come to your family in several milder, negotiable stages before your child enters the final phase, from which there is no return. While "yuck" from a three-, a four-, or even a six-year-old will mean "I'm too old for that," there are plenty of recordings to accommodate their next level of growth.

Listening Moods: Your Growing Child

When your child is very young, you will have to judge for yourself whether the music you have chosen is appropriate for the moment. If it is a peaceful morning and you've chosen a quiet recording to enhance it, is it doing that? You can tell by watching and listening to your baby. Is your newborn sitting or lying peacefully? Is the music helping her doze off to sleep? If it is upbeat, is your infant reacting by smiling, laughing, or moving to the beat? At the other end of the scale, is it making her cry?

A good friend once complained to me that her husband insisted on playing his favorite Rachmaninoff piano concerto in the early evenings just as their preschool-age children were getting ready for bed. Unfortunately, the rousing music often had a negative effect, going so far as to heighten the children's already cranky moods.

Musical Tastes: Yours, Theirs, and Ours

Many adults find that music has the power to relax, inspire, and reaffirm their thoughts and emotions, and they want to share these good feelings with their children. Whether they are classical music buffs, opera lovers, folk music enthusiasts, or rock aficionados, music-loving adults go out of their way to play their favorites for their children in the hope that they will foster in them similar tastes.

Inevitably the time arrives when a child becomes capable of expressing his musical opinions, sometimes rejecting the sounds preferred by his parents in favor of sounds that his parents can't understand. My cousin Melanie, who was raised listening to folk music, was shocked when two-year-old Noah began to cry at the sound of Raffi. She was equally mystified when he requested multiple viewings of a Fred Astaire–Ginger Rogers movie, although she was delighted to comply.

As parents, we may be disappointed or revolted by our children's tastes, yet it is important to acknowledge them. Listening to music is an important area, rooted deep inside of them, where they can experiment with and live out their growing need for autonomy. (Of course, this is easy for me to say. My son, at age eleven, still enjoys sounds that I understand, while the fourteen-year-old children of my friends and relatives are enamored of Metallica, whose music is substantially harder for parents to appreciate.)

Let's remember that we all go through phases in our tastes. Our own musical preferences have evolved over the years. An acid-rock-loving fourteen-year-old may drift back to gentler-sounding music a few years down the road—or the musicality of acid rock may eventually become more apparent to his parents!

Popular Music

Commercial music is the most accessible for family listening; you can listen to the radio together in the car or in the kitchen. With so much air time given over to "oldies," there is remarkable opportunity for adults to share their memories with their fascinated children. Country music is also a popular choice for family listening, because it has a simpler sound than current Top Ten favorites.

Even though my parents have never figured out why it was so appealing, the rock 'n' roll that I loved as a child is now considered classic. By the same token, I have yet to discover what is so appealing about the music adored by Ben, our son's fourteen-year-old baby-sitter. Still, I recognize that Ben and his friends are going through an important process. By establishing their own set of musical tastes, they are exercising their ability to make their own decisions.

However, as a responsible parent who wants to see our children grow up with positive feelings and ethical values, I urge you to seek out pop music that is appropriate to young listeners and supplement your family's listening diet with healthy helpings of music from *All Ears*. Your young children need to hear that it's okay to be different, okay to feel good about themselves, and okay to talk about mean teachers and hating asparagus. The world is a place for everyone, but these days it's hard for our children to understand. Someone's got to clue them in— and that means you.

Understanding the Value of Repetition

During periods of your child's life you will notice that she wants to hear the same books and the same records or tapes over and over and over again. As a "smart" adult, resist the temptation to hamper what you might consider a useless or boring activity. Instead, value these repeat performances. They provide your child with dynamic learning experiences.

By supporting your child's natural instinct for repeated listenings, you are enhancing her ability to develop her own personal system of learning. Don't be discouraged or skeptical because you can't "see" immediate results. Instead, trust your child. A song or album may sound the same to you every time you hear it; but to your child, each listening period is another opportunity to gain mastery of it. By hearing the same music over and over again, she absorbs combinations of tones, rhythms, words, phrases, concepts, and emotions. While your child's ultimate goal is to "master" the tune and the words of a song, a benefit of hearing the same music frequently is that it takes on an importance akin to that of an old friend who offers reassurance and comfort at each meeting.

By giving your child the room for personal and individual growth through repetition, you are also giving her a comforting, secure base from which she will develop the impetus and drive to take on new learning challenges when she senses that the time is right. The development of this invisible personal learning style will be the basis of your child's most meaningful educational experiences.

When I found out that my friends Lisa and Richard were traveling with their children from Long Island to Florida, I gave them a box of fourteen carefully chosen tapes to take along in the car. They are all enthusiastic listeners, and I looked forward to their responses.

When they returned, Lisa was apologetic and more than a little embarrassed. During their two-week trip they had listened to only one tape—over and over and over again. Adam, age five, had fallen in love with Bill Harley's *Dinosaurs Never Say Please.* Amanda, age two, was more than willing to go along with her big brother's taste. While Lisa and Richard, as adults, would have chosen a more diverse listening diet, as parents they had no problem with meeting Adam's request. For one thing, they respected their children's need for repetition, and for another, they really *liked* hearing Bill Harley.

Breaking the Chain of Repetition—Gently

There comes a time when even the most patient parent feels the urge to hear something new. But many children resist all overt efforts their parents make to introduce unfamiliar foods, activities, or music. And when your child is adamant in her refusal to accept something new, it's easy to imagine that her attitude is permanent. In fact, it's not.

Resist the temptation to make the differences of aesthetics between you and your children into a major battle. Children can hold fast to their opinions, no matter how irrational they may seem to us. The harder we push them to accept something new, the firmer they become in their resolve.

Although nothing is forever, when our children are young and resistant it's hard for us to imagine they will ever change their minds. And sometimes, though they outgrow one set of preferences, their tastes remain intrinsically different from ours. But more often, it's just a matter of time before they grow into their ability to enjoy what we are offering.

Every listening situation is personal and different. Described below are techniques to keep in mind when you have a new recording to play for a child who wants to hear only a favorite one.

You will probably have your greatest success if you play your new selection right after the favored one. Or offer to play "just one song" on the new recording because you know it will have special meaning for your child. Tell your child about the song you have in mind for him and explain why you think he will like it.

Introducing Your Children to Music

There are many different ways and times to introduce your children to new music. Read through the following sections with an eye toward finding techniques that you can use or adapt to help your children become adventurous listeners. Experiment to find what works best for you and your family as they grow.

When a baby is newborn it is impossible to predict her musical tastes. In fact, as she grows, her listening needs flower and shift. Be sensitive, enthusiastic, inventive, and patient when you introduce a new recording to your young children. Don't expect everything you play to become an instant favorite, although many recordings become instant family hits for no particular reason.

If your child has a hard time listening at first (and many children do), don't expect him to be able to absorb an entire new album at once. Instead, combine some of the techniques discussed below to help him "grow" into his listening abilities.

Resist forcing unwelcome listening on your children, but don't give up trying to find what they like and when they like it. Finding the magic combination can take work, but it's worth the effort. By helping your children become well-rounded listeners, you are encouraging them to grow into thoughtful, well-spoken, well-focused people.

Be Sensitive

Sensitivity to your child's mood is especially important at the moment you want to introduce a recording. By respecting her feelings and tailoring your musical "offering" to what you think your child will receive, you will increase your chances of success.

If your child is cranky, it's unlikely that she will relax enough to appreciate hearing something new. Cranky times are usually the times for soothing old listening favorites. If your child is of preschool age, you might find out from her teacher what she is enjoying at school and where you can buy it. Keep "old faithful" recordings on hand for moments when nothing new will do.

If your young child is in a rough-and-tumble mood, you probably won't have much success if you try to introduce her to the mellow sounds of Kevin Roth or Raffi. Depending on her age, you would do better to try out Tom Glazer or ROSENSHONTZ. That's not to say it can't be done. Anything can happen if you are sensitive and enthusiastic.

If it's morning or a sunny day, you might try out something upbeat. If you feel your child would benefit from a perky sound (such as right after a nap), energetic sounds are also appropriate.

Quiet, comforting sounds may be more appealing in the afternoon or before bedtime or a nap. While comforting sounds may also be appropriate on a rainy day when you're all stuck inside, more active sounds may offer just the distraction your family needs to get through an endless afternoon.

Gentle yet upbeat sounds are also good choices for times when your child is confined indoors. Children who are recuperating from an illness are particularly receptive listeners, because they have usually reached their saturation point with TV and storybooks and are eager for something else.

Be Enthusiastic!

If you play a recording that you really like, your child will sense it. Your enthusiasm will be contagious.

At first you will instinctively play for your child what you like listening to best. But the time will come when you are ready, for your child's sake, to experiment with listening to "kids' music." To identify music in a style that you enjoy, read through chapter 6.

Whenever possible, listen to a new recording before you play it for your child. By becoming familiar with its sound and content, you will be able to cheer your child through his first listening session.

If in the process of listening you develop a favorite song or hear a song about a favorite subject of your child's, be sure to tell him about it before you listen together. He might not be interested in listening to a new album until you tell him about the great dinosaur song that's on it.

Hunt for Old Favorites

Since enthusiasm is such an important aspect of music listening, you may want to put serious effort into unearthing some of your old favorites to share with your family.

Start in your own backyard. Ask your parents if they have your old records stored away. I was amazed to discover that my otherwise "throw it away" mother still had a stack of my old favorites stowed away (and that cousins living nearby still had my electric trains). She gave them to me gleefully, delighted to empty out the shelf in the closet at long last.

As I heard my childhood favorites for the first time in thirty-five years, my scratchy old records sounded great to me. It was hard not to be enthusiastic when I played them for Jesse. Many he grew to love (much to my satisfaction), though with some he never connected. Sharing my childhood music with him got us off to a great start. I wish you all the same joy!

Of course, the chances are slim that you'll recover your old records so easily, but don't give up the search. While many terrific recordings have unfortunately gone out of print, a surprising number of classics—records by the Weavers and Pete Seeger, Mary Martin's *Peter Pan* and Danny Kaye's *Hans Christian Andersen*— are currently available through catalogues and in well-stocked record stores. Your local library may have copies of your old favorites, or it may be able to get you a copy through interlibrary borrowing systems.

Yard sales, garage sales, white elephants, and school fairs are other surprising sources for old favorites. You may not get your favorite *Herman Ermine in Rabbit Town* in pristine condition, but you might be amazed at, for twenty-five cents, just how good it sounds.

Find the Compromise

Any combination of "ifs" could work for you and your children, but you have to watch carefully for their responses. If your children are clearly uncomfortable with the music that you are playing, consider making a compromise offer.

The first time I put on a Pete Seeger record for my son, Jesse, then two and a half, he put his fingers in his ears and shrieked until I turned it off. I thought my heart would break! Pete Seeger is America's greatest folk singer, and I had been raised on his music. I put the record away, and I didn't think of it again for more than a year.

But as Jesse neared his fourth birthday, he developed a fascination with trains. We began reading train stories, riding trains, visiting train museums, and building trains out of blocks. One rainy afternoon I suddenly remembered that "Wabash Cannon Ball" was on the Pete Seeger album that Jesse had rejected. I pulled it out, and of course, at first sight, Jesse didn't want any part of it.

"Just listen to this one great train song and then we'll turn it off," I suggested. I was delighted when he agreed.

After being clearly annoyed and then merely disinterested in that "one great song," he asked to hear it again a few days later, and then again the day after that. Within a month "Wabash Cannon Ball" had become a favorite. Eventually he asked to hear the rest of the side, and then the rest of the recording. Soon he developed a few more favorites on the album, until he began feeling attached to the whole thing.

Dealing with Repetition

You can guess what happened next. Jesse wanted to hear *Pete Seeger's American Folk Songs* every day, sometimes more than once. I have a high tolerance for repeated listenings (that's how I came to want to write this book), but Jesse could outlast me. That's when we discovered the importance of the child-oriented cassette player.

At four years old Jesse was ready to sit by himself and listen to his favorite music or story. He used the Fisher-Price record player and later their tape machine. (It was 1982, and cassettes were just becoming popular.) (For more, see "Audio Equipment for Kids," page 30.)

Negotiating Family Tastes and Distastes

If you have several young children, you will have the most success if you play music that appeals to the oldest. Even if it is slightly above their comprehension, the younger ones are usually thrilled to listen to something appreciated by an older sibling. On the other hand, there are a remarkable number of recordings available that have the ability to span the ages. You may find that your eight-year-old, three-year-old, and you can all enjoy the same music. But your enthusiasm and sensitivity will be all-important when it comes time to get children of diverse ages to focus for the first time on the same recording.

Of course, the moment will arrive when each child will want to hear his or her favorite recording. Since this could signal the outbreak of a world war in your home or car, act fast to assure each child that he or she will get equal access to the airwaves. Whenever possible, encourage each objecting child to find something, no matter how small, to enjoy in the selection on hand. When all else fails, consider letting one child use a Walkman-style tape player to resolve the listening conflict.

While the basic premise of *All Ears* is that families benefit from listening to music together, as your children reach their late elementary years—and especially during car rides—a cassette player with a headset can make the difference between war and peace.

Audio Equipment for Kids

Use a birthday celebration or major holiday as reason to purchase a child-oriented cassette player for your three- or four-year-old. In addition to Fisher-Price, many of the audio companies, such as Panasonic, General Electric, and Sony, are making well-padded machines with simple, oversized control buttons. While their sound quality is far from state-of-the-art, it is often remarkably good, and your child will get a lot of pleasure and a feeling of empowerment out of being able to operate her own machine. The gift of a kids' tape player can be particularly important if there's a new baby in the house who is taking over the spotlight or for a young child who wants to emulate an older sibling.

High-Quality Audio Equipment

If you have high-quality sound equipment in your home or car, be sure to play your children's favorite recordings for them to hear. While it's a mistake to deprive your child of the chance to operate her own child-oriented cassette player because your own ears are sensitized to higher fidelity, it's a treat for them to hear the richer sound when it is available.

As your children grow older, you will be tempted to buy them more sophisticated equipment. While you might think this a sign of superior parenting, the reality not only can be expensive but can cause unnecessary conflict between parents and child.

I bought Jesse a substantially better, Walkman-style cassette player when he was six. Within several weeks he had dropped it several times. It was lamentably defunct. By age nine he had demolished several. (Replacing them may have been foolishness on my part, but they're invaluable on long trips.) His most creative atrocity was to lose the plastic piece that held the batteries in place. For months he used masking tape.

For his tenth birthday Jesse's grandparents bought him a new sports-oriented cassette player with the idea that it would stand up to abuse. Jesse is eleven, and unless he just hasn't confessed, at this writing it is still working.

Too Much Listening?

It's hard to imagine that your children can overdo listening to tapes. Every minute that they listen is another minute that they focus on language, rhythm, melody and create invisible pictures for themselves. When they listen carefully, they use their imaginations. When they use the music as background sound, they are being relaxed and reassured by it.

If you play music in your home constantly, you run the risk of having it transform into background sound as opposed to music for listening. On the other hand, if you are one of those people who likes to have constant background noise in your life, good-quality music is a hundred times better than the empty chaos of the television or commercial radio, which so many people are in the habit of playing.

It is my personal experience that the rhythm and texture of good "background" music stays with me even after I leave it, helping me get through many uninspiring tasks. But then, I am one of those weirdos whom you notice humming in the supermarket.

Your children *can* spend too much time listening through headsets, however. Prolonged music listening at such close range, especially if the music is too loud, can do lasting damage to the listener's ears.

The Dos and Don'ts of Listening

DON'T play a recording once, decide that you or your child hates it, and throw it away. Instead, find a compromise. There are so many elements that go into listening that it would be a shame to shortchange yourself, your family, and the recording.

DO introduce your child to one song that has special meaning to him. Look for songs that are about specific topics of special interest. Choose a song related to something already in your child's experience or something in which he has a particular interest. You might say, "Listen to this great dinosaur song," or "Wait until you hear how some kids help their mother in the kitchen—I'm not too sure if she likes it."

DON'T interrupt your child if he is happily involved doing something else. He will come to resent music listening times.

DO add another dimension to a quiet activity by putting on music while you and your children play with wood or Lego blocks or clay, draw, paint, or do a puzzle.

DO seize the moment if your child comes to you asking you to suggest something to do. Play upbeat, energetic music as an accompaniment to a hands-on activity such as the ones listed above. Activity recordings are also ideal when you and your young child are in search of entertainment. Choose a recording that is age appropriate to your child.

DO consider mealtime for listening. If mealtime has become a battle time, you may want to create a truce by playing a recording you can all enjoy instead of hassling over food issues. (For humorous eating songs, look to ROSENSHONTZ, Barry Louis Polisar, David Polansky, and "Weird Al" Yankovic.)

DO make car-riding times music listening times. The car is the perfect place for family listening, so either have your car equipped with a cassette player or bring along a portable machine. Although group listening can be a lot of fun for everyone, consider allowing warring siblings to use personal cassette players during long trips.

DO supervise your children's use of Walkman-type cassette players. Be sure that they keep the volume low. If your child cannot hear your normal speaking voice over the sounds coming through the headset, it's too loud. Sustained listening to loud music can permanently damage their ears.

DON'T allow your children to walk on the street listening to headsets, no matter what their ages. Sounds plugged directly into their ears block out auditory cues that will protect them from accidents. Also, Walkman-style cassette players block out the world itself. It's vital that your children stay in touch with the myriad sounds around them.

DO encourage your children to develop their own musical tastes. It will give them a good sense of their ability to make decisions.

DO identify what your children like to hear. Keep them supplied with a variety of quality, age-appropriate listening material. (See chapter 6, beginning on page 59.)

Important Listening Treats

What Is "Live Music"?

In *All Ears* I use the words "live music" to describe a gamut of listening experiences, from hearing the simple sound of a spoon tapping against a glass to absorbing the earth-moving crescendos of a symphony orchestra. I include as worthwhile "live music" experiences the sounds your child hears when she experiments at the piano keyboard or the "music" you produce for your child as you stumble through a simple folk tune on the guitar.

Encourage your child to listen and experiment with a variety of basic sounds. Don't underrate the value for your child of "playing" at music making or hearing and seeing music being performed in front of her, no matter how primitive the performance. By the time your child enters her early elementary years (if you haven't begun earlier), be sure to provide her with plenty of opportunities to hear music performed by skilled musicians.

Setting the Time for Concertgoing

Hearing masterfully performed live music in concert is a unique experience that nurtures and stimulates people at every age, provided the listener is relaxed and willing. While some parents feel comfortable, even driven, to take their infants to concerts as soon as they are born, others wait until their children are toddlers. Some parents, never quite figuring out what is the "right time," neglect the concertgoing aspect of their children's lives completely.

Of course, you will follow the timetable that is most comfortable for you; but if you look to avoid early concertgoing experiences altogether, reconsider! Positive early experiences will have lasting benefits for your growing child—and for you.

Read through the following section, which offers you realistic guidelines for helping your child become an accomplished "audience." The key here is to understand that while early listening experiences can have long-term impact on your child's ability to appreciate and understand music, negative concertgoing experiences may leave an enduring bad taste. If you take concertgoing slow and easy, as an unexpected bonus it will become one of your most beloved family activities.

Infants as Audiences

Most infants are lulled to sleep by the full sounds of a symphonic composition filling the concert hall, and that's appropriate. If your baby is unnerved by the sound, however, it is only reasonable that you will remove her from the auditorium, both for her own comfort and for the comfort of those around you.

Toddlers and Preschoolers as Audiences

If you are assuming that you will be able to take your toddler or preschooler into a theater for the first time, plop him into a seat, and have him sit silently through an entire performance of *The Nutcracker,* think again. Children are not born knowing how to be an audience. They learn through your encouragement and guidance and through their own positive experiences. For help, read on.

Elementary-Age Children as Audiences

High quality, in-school performances are geared toward helping children to develop their maturing listening skills. Although we hope that all elementary schools offer children the opportunity to see and hear music being performed, sadly, in this age of cutbacks and austerity school budgets, we cannot take this assumption for granted.

Speak with your principal or Parent-Teacher Association chairperson to learn what performances have been scheduled in your child's school. If you are invited to suggest names of appropriate in-school performers, do not hesitate to cite your child's favorite recording artist or artists. Offer to provide further information.

Whether you merely want to suggest a few names to your local school principal or children's librarian or are willing to get involved bringing listening opportunities to a school where there are none, your elementary-age children will benefit from your involvement in their music listening activities.

How to Make a Live Performance a Great Listening Experience for Your Child

When it comes to raising an enthusiastic music listener, you are your child's perfect teacher. Though it's a subtle, sometimes frustrating process which will require you to marshal large helpings of patience and flexibility, overall, if your child has a good time at a concert without disturbing those around him, you are succeeding in your goal of providing good listening experiences.

Please remember: while your child is being enchanted by the music, he is having a constructive listening experience. However, the positives of your child's concert experience can be easily negated by memories of being forced to sit still. Remind yourself of this when you are trying to overcome the frustration of being obliged to leave a concert early. And please always be considerate of those sitting around you who expect and deserve to hear the music without distraction. For more on this, see "Be flexible," page 42.

Be Selfless

Choose a concert for your child to attend solely because you believe she will enjoy it. If you are more excited about hearing James Galway or the Beach Boys give a once-in-a-lifetime performance in your town than you are about your child having a positive experience, leave your child home. On the other hand, it is better for you both to hear twenty magical minutes of Pavarotti or Raffi than never to have heard them at all.

If you can't resist taking your child to hear a performance that has a special meaning for you, consider bringing along an extra adult (such as a baby-sitter, a spouse, a grandparent, or a friend) who is prepared to leave the concert early with your child. (See "Be well staffed," page 42.)

Adults as Beginning Listeners

You will most likely take your child to hear music with which you already have a fond familiarity. However, if classical music has not yet become a part of your life, remember, it's never too late for either of you to become listeners. Let the impetus come from wanting to do the best for your child. You will get double the pleasure if you discover music together.

Choosing a Familiar Ballet or Opera

If your child has danced to a selection of music from *The Nutcracker* or *The Magic Flute* at home or in preschool, look for professional and school productions of these classics in your community. Be sure to listen to a complete recording at home in small segments before the event and discuss the story together, as described below.

If, however, you would like to take your child to a performance of a ballet or opera that he has not yet seen or heard, there are many lovely ways of making them familiar.

Choose an opera or ballet with a story line that is simple enough for your child to grasp. Explain the story ahead of time. While your child will enjoy hearing you recount the tale in your own words and style, you may want to follow up your interpretation with additional material.

Libraries, bookstores, and catalogues offer picture books that describe and illustrate musical classics such as *Peter and the Wolf, Hansel and Gretel, Amahl and the Night Visitors,* and *The Firebird.* The printed story is bound to vary slightly from your version. Be sure your child understands that tales are always subject to variation! If you are unfamiliar with the story, be sure to read it alone first to decide whether it is appropriate for your child.

Check libraries, video rental stores, public-television listings, and the libraries of friends for videotaped performances of musical classics. Watch the tape in small segments with your child. Take advantage of videotape capabilities by freezing the action to explain what he will hear in an upcoming segment, or replay a musical passage to help reinforce it.

Introducing Your Child to Concertgoing

Before you spring for tickets to a concert or an opera, you will want to prepare your child (and yourself) through a variety of activities. For starters, consider taking your child to a smaller-scale performance. Check your newspapers, local library bulletins, and parenting publications for simpler, more intimate performances that involve just a few instruments and voices. Take your child to hear performances given by schoolchildren and by community and church bands, orchestras, and choruses.

Most important, no matter who is giving the performance, listen together to a recorded version in several small helpings during the weeks or days before the event. Let your child see how much you enjoy listening. It's always appropriate to hum or sing along and to move and make up your own dances together while listening together at home. If you are already familiar with the music, point out your favorite passages and themes. Reminisce about your concertgoing or listening experiences.

To help your preschooler understand that different sounds emanate from different kinds of instruments, arrive at the concert early enough to hear the instruments being tuned. Be sure to point out the individual instruments that you both can see. Help your child identify the specific sounds made by each instrument as you hear them. Even if your elementary-age child, who may be having firsthand exposure to instruments in school, tells you, "I already know that," she will still benefit from your dialogue. It takes time to absorb the concept that an orchestra is made up of the sounds of a variety of instruments blending and weaving together.

In Praise of Family Concerts

There is no more energizing or constructive way to spend an hour with your children than to listen, sing, laugh, clap, and swing together at a family concert.

The family concert experience will unite your family in unique harmony through mutual enjoyment and understanding.

Your child may develop a favorite contemporary recording artist by hearing recorded music or by seeing a concert on television or videotape. Many of these performers tour the country giving performances in schools, libraries, and concert halls.

Famous Performers and Recording Artists

Through the powerful exposure of television and video, some children's recording artists have become household names. When Raffi or Sharon, Lois and Bram announce their tour locations, their concerts sell out overnight. I, for one, have missed a few chances to take my son to hear them because the tickets were long sold out by the time I called the box office.

If you notice in the paper or learn through word of mouth that your child's favorite performer is appearing nearby, I urge you to act fast in buying tickets. There is nothing more exciting than seeing a beloved recording artist perform— and nothing more frustrating than discovering that you have missed the opportunity.

Not-So-Famous Performers and Recording Artists

Don't pass up the opportunity to hear a contemporary children's performer because you are unfamiliar with his or her name. Tickets to concerts given by lesser-known yet highly talented and innovative artists are often more readily available merely because major media exposure has not yet transformed these people into superstars in your neighborhood. Although fame for many children's performers often remains regional, composers and performers continue to create innovative, meaningful work despite their lack of national celebrity.

If you see that a not-so-famous (or downright unknown) children's performer will be giving a concert in your area, take a few minutes to find out from the concert sponsor or ticket distributor if the performance will be age appropriate for your child. While toddlers may be fascinated by music geared for five-to-nine-year-olds, your seven-year-old may be mortified if he finds himself at a performance geared to two-year-olds.

Whenever possible, listen with your child to the recordings of a performer you are to see in advance of the concert. Hearing familiar music in concert has its own special pleasure. It takes only a few listenings for music to become comfortable. Concert sponsors will be able to help you locate recordings.

On the other hand, don't pass up the opportunity to take your child to an age-appropriate concert merely because she is unfamiliar with the music. Skilled family performers know how to draw listeners into their music quickly through sing-alongs and other forms of audience participation. As a result, their music doesn't remain "new" for very long.

Buying a Recording at a Concert

Consider buying a recording at the concert if it is offered for sale. With tune fragments buzzing around in your head for hours or even days afterward, you are bound to wish you could hear some of those songs again. You may discover too late that the recording you want is not stocked in your local music store.

When the recording you purchase after a concert becomes a favorite in your household, ask your local music or book store to order a few copies for you to purchase as birthday and holiday gifts for friends and relatives.

What Parents Should Know About Concertgoing with Children

Be realistic. Be considerate.

Before going to the concert, distinguish tactfully for your child the difference between listening activities at home and listening manners at a concert. Describe concert listening in an upbeat, positive light, explaining what it means to be a good audience.

Be careful not to overwhelm your child with unrealistic restrictions. While your child will need to sit patiently through a symphony, opera, or ballet, performances geared to young listeners offer the opportunity to clap, sing, and dance along.

If your child is sitting quietly (or is otherwise appropriately involved with the music) and the child in the next seat, or even five rows back, is whining or crying, wouldn't you want the parent to remove the unhappy child from the audience? Others expect the same consideration from you and your family. And really, it is much more constructive for *everyone* for you to acquiesce to your child's request to leave before she becomes disruptive.

Be flexible.

The first time your child tells you she is ready to leave, you might try to forestall her with a small, noiseless treat such as a favorite bear to cuddle or a piece of candy to suck quietly; but beyond a certain point it is more advantageous to trust your child's instincts. Encourage your child's enthusiasm for music to grow on a foundation of happy memories rather than douse her emerging interest by forcing her to sit beyond her endurance.

Be well staffed.

If you are taking two or more young children to a concert, take two adults—one to stay in the concert, one to take the bathroom or lobby detail. To avoid conflict and bad feelings, discuss ahead which adult will assume which responsibilities! My husband was a marvelous sport at several concerts that we attended when our son was young, removing Jesse at the moment appropriate for Jesse, leaving me to hear the rest of the music.

Locating Live Performances in Your Community

Professional concert promoters, school arts councils, church groups, folk music societies, historical societies, museums, arts festivals, not-for-profit organizations, nursery schools, and bookstores sponsor family concerts. Keep yourself on the lookout for newspaper announcements and publicity articles as well as posters hanging in shop windows, libraries, and schools.

Indicate to your friends in nearby areas that you and your children are interested in going to family concerts so that they will let you know when their school or local theater announces a special event. If not for a casual conversation about kids' music that I had with a friend in New York City several years ago, my family and I would have missed a rare opportunity to catch Tom Glazer in concert.

Locating Performances of a Favorite Artist

If your child has developed a passion for the music of Bill Harley, Marcy Marxer, Barry Louis Polisar, Raffi, or any other performer, you may not want to leave your concertgoing activities to chance. Instead, drop a note to the recording distributor or management company noted on the recording. Sometimes the artist is also the distributor. It may take a few letters or phone calls, but ultimately you will find a person to send you a list of concert locations and dates.

Don't be discouraged from contacting an artist because the address on the album is halfway across the country from you. Some artists are distributed by companies in Chicago or Albany when in fact they live and perform in Washington, D.C., or Los Angeles.

Some artists undertake national tours, while others limit their performance locations to those within several hours' drive of their home. By obtaining a concert schedule, you may be delighted to discover that your favorite artist is appearing in your town or in a nearby city.

Many recording artists—including Tom Paxton, Sally Rogers, Barry Louis Polisar, Bill Harley, and Frank Cappelli—publish their own newsletters which contain, in addition to their concert schedules, personal anecdotes and insights that will help you and your family get to know them better. Other artists—such as Marcy Marxer, Cathy Fink, John McCutcheon, Jim Valley, and Janice Buckner—publish activity booklets that will enhance your family's enjoyment of their albums.

Bringing a Performing Artist to Your Community

If you know of a school, library, cultural arts council, church, or other community group that offers performances for families, or if you know of an organization or theater that schedules these kinds of events, don't hesitate to contact the director or person in charge of programming with names of performers whose recordings you and your family enjoy hearing. Or you may want to approach a child-centered organization that has not previously sponsored a family concert and get involved organizing one yourself.

There are many positive reasons for you to bring a favorite artist to your community. In addition to creating a dynamic family event that can be enjoyed by a wide range of people, you can create public awareness and stimulate fund-raising for a worthy child-oriented organization. In addition, you will come together with other adults within your community who appreciate the importance of family interaction.

Best of all, you and your family will enjoy hearing, meeting, and getting to know the performers. It will be an experience that everyone will long remember.

When it comes to running a concert, performers and their managers will be able to guide you in a variety of ways. They know a great deal about the availability of funding, grants, and sponsorship for family concerts, so be sure to ask about this.

Managers or publicists may be willing to furnish you with a publicity release. At the very least, they will furnish you with photographs and biographical material about the artist.

Radio for Children

Doing battle with the evil forces of homogenized commercial radio that dominate the airways, more and more radio shows for kids are popping up on independent stations around the country. Radio programming for kids is not really new; it's just experiencing a renaissance. Some shows are already veterans. Uncle Ruthie's "Half Way Down the Stairs" has been on the air since 1970, and P. J. Swift's "Pickleberry Pie" has been in syndication since 1986.

Imaginative programs for children, which are aired primarily on public and university-sponsored radio stations, are hosted by caring, intelligent people who are committed to the premise that quality radio listening improves children's concentration, listening skills, and self-esteem. Inspired by radio's glorious past and motivated by the avalanche of innovative music, storytelling, and drama recordings available for children, the producers of radio for children know that young listeners benefit from good listening both now, while they are young, and later, when they are grown.

Many producers, themselves parents or grandparents, are tuned in to innovative ways of communicating with young audiences. By letting kids do the hosting and news reporting themselves, by broadcasting call-in and interview shows specifically for sophisticated young audiences, they encourage active participation from children.

Whether you discover a wonderful program for your family as you are twirling the radio dial in a desperate search for something "different," or tune in to a kids' show for the first time because you've learned about it through word of mouth, a listing in the paper, or here in *All Ears,* you and your children will be delighted with what you hear.

While trying to list *all* radio shows for children is akin to aiming at a moving target, a partial list of shows across the country appears in the Parents' Resource Guide, beginning on page 195. Since times and days change frequently, call the station in your area for up-to-date information.

Again, as discussed earlier, age appropriateness should be a major factor when selecting a program for family listening. While younger children may be delighted with the upbeat programming aimed at their older siblings, six- or seven-year-olds will probably have little patience for a show geared to their preschool brothers and sisters.

Making Musical Selections

Before we buy a book for our child, we can turn the pages in the bookstore to get a taste of the language and the style of illustration. While we can't accurately predict whether our child will like the book, we can make an educated guess, which, paired with our own enthusiasm, will go a long way toward assuring our child's acceptance of our purchase.

Until listening booths are revived in our local record and book shops (and I know this is in fact beginning to happen), it remains impossible for us to hear the language and musical style of a recording until we get it home. We must make a judgment based on the cover art and liner notes and keep our fingers crossed that we aren't throwing ten dollars out the window.

To give us a little more guidance and reassurance, some well-intentioned distributors are now printing age recommendations on the outside of the packages. These figures can be good jumping-off points for making decisions, but I have discovered that we should treat them as flexible estimates.

There are many elements that affect whether or not a child will "like" a particular recording. Numbers can't tell the whole story. To help you pick winners when choosing recordings for your family, I offer the following observations.

Timing

Children, like adults, have different tastes for sound at different times of the day as well as at different stages of their lives. What holds little appeal to your child at eighteen months may become a cherished recording when he's twenty-two months or thirty-six months. If your child is disinterested or annoyed by a recording the first time you play it for him, put it away for the moment.

Respecting Differences of Taste

Examine age-appeal recommendations and descriptive overviews in terms of your own tastes and the tastes and interests of your children. Don't forget that each child is capable of having dramatically different taste. Your firstborn may have had no use for Raffi, while your second child may find him irresistible. Your third child may have a passion for bluegrass music that you never saw in the other two.

In the case of a class of schoolchildren, be sure to assess the interests and development of the group as a whole. Seek out musical selections that coordinate with a specific unit in your curriculum. Every child in the class may not be instantly captivated by your choice of music; but your enthusiasm, enhanced by the endorsement of some of the class members, will go far in winning over the attention, if not the respect, of others in the group. In some cases, children don't like a song or a piece of music the first time they hear it merely because it is so foreign to anything they have ever heard before. A few listening sessions with your enthusiastic comments about the music will help ease them into the new sounds.

Interpreting Age-Appeal Recommendations

An age-appeal recommendation does not mean that all children between those ages will love all recordings designated in that category. It means instead that the material included on those recordings is suitable for children between those ages.

Many recordings are given broad age-appeal recommendations by their producers. In many cases the designated ranges, such as "two and up" or "three to eleven" (and, of course, "3 to 103") are too wide to be realistic. Even the age recommendation of three to eight is common; yet a three-year-old and an eight-year-old have very different agendas.

Target Ages

In some instances I have added a secondary rating which describes the "target age" of the listener. Based on the concepts, vocabulary, and musical style heard on a recording, the target age may be a better indication of the ideal age for a first-time listener.

Raffi's *Corner Grocery Store* and *Rise and Shine* are designated for listeners from "three to eight," while his *Baby Beluga* and *One Light, One Sun* are recommended for listeners "three to adult." The "three to eight" recordings contain simple, repetitive nursery rhymes that are more realistically targeted at children from three to five. The recordings designated "three to adult," while really targeted at three-to-six-year-olds, contain songs with universal messages (such as the title songs, "Baby Beluga" and "One Light, One Sun") that make them appropriate for pre-school and early-elementary classroom use. They have a gentle, classic sound that also makes them appealing to newborns and adults. As always, personal preference will be an important factor.

Bill Harley's recordings are targeted at various ages. *Dinosaurs Never Say Please* and *Monsters in the Bathroom* are really meant for five-to-eight-year-olds, while *You're in Trouble* is targeted at six-to-nine-year-olds, and *Cool in School* is meant for nine-to-twelve-year-olds. This does not mean that your five-year-old won't enjoy listening to *Cool in School* along with her older sibling, but the social issues and situations that are described on the recording are still beyond the range of her experience.

Mary Miché's recordings, though tagged as age appropriate three to eleven, are more specifically targeted at five-to-eight-year-olds. On the other hand, there is both a clarity and a singability that make Mary's recordings appropriate for some three-year-olds and an underlying sophistication of language and information that makes them, especially *Earthy Tunes,* appropriate for classroom use with older elementary-age children and adults.

When a Recording Becomes "Babyish"

Keep in mind that there is a big difference between a six-year-old who is hearing a recording for the first time and a six-year-old who is continuing to enjoy a recording that she has been listening to and enjoying for several years. If you present your child a recording designated "three and up" on her sixth birthday, you are certain to be wasting your money. On the other hand, a child who has been listening to that same recording since age three or four may still find great comfort in hearing it when she's six.

At around seven or eight (or sometimes, sadly, sooner) children take on a new worldliness that interferes with their ability to enjoy things that they consider "babyish." Identifying just what is "babyish" to them is tricky, though you can be sure that anything they hear on MTV or commercial radio becomes eminently acceptable when ROSENSHONTZ suddenly is not.

An Extra Effort Toward Older Children

If your children have been raised on a varied diet of musical styles, they'll stay open to hearing new music longer than if they have grown up on a steady diet of commercial radio and television. But don't try to bludgeon them with selections from *All Ears* if, at ages six or eight, they are already hooked on commercial radio. Instead, read through the descriptions in chapter 6 to identify their interests. Your sensitivity, patience, and enthusiasm will be especially important if your children are to open their ears to sounds that are both musically more gentle and verbally more demanding than what they are used to hearing.

Where to Find Recordings

The children's department of your local library is the first place to check for family-listening recordings. Borrowing records and tapes from the library has the advantage of being risk free. If you and your child don't like what you hear, you can simply return the recording to the library.

Of course there are also several drawbacks. Your library may not have an in-depth collection of recordings from which to choose. Or the recording you borrow may be in dismal condition. Finally, you have to return the recording just as it's becoming a favorite.

Start at your neighborhood library, but once you get excited about family listening, expand your musical horizons by purchasing your own records, tapes, or CDs.

Buying Recordings Locally

Of course, you would expect that music for family listening would be available in your neighborhood record store. And some of it is. You may have a chain store that carries only a few nationally distributed titles, or you may be lucky enough to have an independently owned music shop that stocks a wide selection of family-listening recordings on a variety of labels. But more likely, you have a bookstore, a toy store, a kids' clothing shop, or even a gift shop whose owner has discovered the magic of family music.

There are several ways to find out who in your community sells recordings for children. First, ask other people. You may have a friend or your child may have a teacher who can point you in the right direction. Or you can browse through your local parenting magazine (see pages 192–95) for names of businesses advertising that they sell recorded music for family listening. A family concert can be a good place to buy a recording as well.

Locating Specific Recordings

If you read about a recording in *All Ears* that you would like to purchase and your local music or book shop can't obtain it for you, write to the artist directly to find out what store in your area carries it or what catalog sells it. Artists who distribute their own recordings will send you an order form in the return mail.

Catalogs

Mail-order catalogs that offer recordings for family listening are proliferating to the point where you might think that if you've seen one, you've seen them all. However, if you are the parent, relative, friend, teacher, or librarian of children, it's worth having several. Each catalog has a distinct personality and offers unusual recordings that you are not likely to find elsewhere. While there is some overlap in the offerings, it is interesting to see who offers what and to read the reasons why. Because many of the catalogs are independent enterprises which grew out of their owners' determination to provide top-notch materials for families and schools (the kind of "low volume" business shunned by "big business"), the listings are often accompanied by well-thought-out, highly personal commentary. Reading a variety of overviews will help you when it comes time to make a decision, especially if you've never heard the recording or artist before.

Making Selections from Catalogs

Just because you see a recording listed here in *All Ears* or in one of the catalogs listed below, it doesn't mean that you or your children will like it. However, you can train yourself to "read between the lines" when you browse through the listings. Look for key words that will tip you off to your family's tastes and needs. Does your three-year-old love to sing and dance? If so, look toward recordings that are designated great preschool sing-alongs. The music offered is chosen and performed within a range appropriate for young children.

Are dinosaurs a fixation of your five-year-old? If so, look for recordings that have great dinosaur songs. Is your six-year-old so tuned in to commercial television and radio that it's already hard to reach him? Look toward recordings that are described as having a full, sophisticated, or contemporary sound.

Are your children always squabbling with each other? If so, look for recordings that deal with family issues. Do you have a shy child, or a child who may be overshadowed by other family members? Do you have a child with disabilities? Is your child afraid of monsters? Is he struggling to learn to ride his bike? If so, look for recordings that help children address these issues. Do you want to help your children avoid sexual abuse? There are several songs geared to help children understand their right to control their own bodies.

Is your fifth grader a great procrastinator or an independent thinker? If so, there are some terrific recordings available for her.

Also, be sure to read carefully the section earlier in this chapter about making choices that are age appropriate.

We want to increase the chances that you and your family end up with recordings that are right for you so that we can bring you back for more.

Catalog Addresses

A Gentle Wind
Box 3103
Albany, NY 12203
(518) 436-0391

With a modest catalog compared with some of those listed below, A Gentle Wind is playing an important part in the current evolution in music for children. Using the folk and jazz traditions, artists on this label cross over into contemporary sounds and songs that address family topics, interests, and activities. Founded in 1981, A Gentle Wind produces and distributes nearly forty original music and storytelling tapes, a remarkable number of which have received awards and commendations from the American Library Association and *Parents' Choice.*

While its recordings are increasingly available in book and record shops and through specialty catalogs, be sure to write for A Gentle Wind's own delightfully illustrated, understated catalog. Through it you will be able to order four remarkably inexpensive sampler tapes which serve as catalogs-to-their-catalog. All titles carry age-appropriate designations for children between the ages of one and twelve.

Sincere in its mission to get good listening to children, A Gentle Wind discounts its recordings—available on cassette only—when purchased directly. To encourage parents and teachers to provide children with hands-on music-listening opportunities (i.e., a child-oriented cassette player and a quiet place to listen), it offers many reassuring (not to mention astonishing) guarantees in the back of its catalog. If a tape is defective, A Gentle Wind will, of course, replace it. But the company will also replace a tape if you deem it inappropriate for your child or if it meets its demise through an accident.

Alcazar's Kiddie Cat
P.O. Box 429
Waterbury, VT 05676
(802) 244-8657

With more than eighty jam-packed pages of listings, photographs, kids' drawings, and ads, Alcazar's Kiddie Cat is the largest catalog of children's music recordings and videos that I've yet seen. Each listing is accompanied by a cheerful overview of the recording and a photo of the cassette or album's cover art. At the back of the catalog you'll find photos of many leading artists with a quote from each about his or her music. For an exciting glimpse of the latest in family listening, take a look through the Kiddie Cat.

Children's Book and Music Center

2500 Santa Monica Blvd.
Santa Monica, CA 90404
(213) 829-0215; toll-free outside California: (800) 443-1856

If you live in or plan to visit southern California, be sure to visit the Children's Book and Music Center in Santa Monica. Barring the opportunity to visit, write for its eighty-page catalog of books, recordings, and videos for home and school. Organized by age appropriateness for infants through eight-year-olds, its offerings cover an impressively wide range: lullaby music, activity recordings, cross-cultural music and classical music, songbooks, musical instruments, and parenting guides are all thoughtfully represented.

The Children's Book and Music Center has created an innovative music previewing service that you can use from anywhere in the country using a touch-tone telephone. Twenty-four hours a day, by calling (213) 385-5312 and listening for instructions, you can hear samples of new and longtime favorite songs from recordings that are age appropriate for your child.

Children's Small Press Collection

719 N. Fourth Ave.
Ann Arbor, MI 48104
(313) 668-8056

The Children's Small Press Collection represents nearly one hundred small publishers whose books and recordings focus on contemporary children's issues; its catalog is an excellent resource guide for parents as well as family and educational support professionals. The material in this collection has been gathered to help adults enhance children's lives through communication and sharing. Addressing issues of cultural diversity, problem solving, and the changing family, the catalog lists fine and difficult-to-locate books and recordings which support the development of self-esteem, responsible behavior, and creative and critical thinking skills of children.

Chinaberry Book Service
2830 Via Orange Way, Suite B
Spring Valley, CA 92078-1521
(800) 777-5205

The Chinaberry Book Service catalog, offering books and music for children and families, is a lovingly assembled creation to savor at your leisure. Since the service was founded in 1980, its catalog has grown to include more than ninety charmingly illustrated newsprint pages of books, recordings, videotapes, and miscellany for parents and their children from birth to fourteen.

In addition to offering unusual and superb products, all organized according to age appropriateness, Chinaberry accompanies each listing with a chatty, personal anecdote describing why the product has been included.

In the back of the catalog are useful subdivisions to help bewildered customers identify their needs and interests. "Baby," "Bedtime," "Siblings," "Gift Ideas for Families with New Babies," "Perfect for Trips," and "Strong Females" are some of the headings.

Educational Activities, Inc.
P.O. Box 87
Baldwin, NY 11510
(516) 223-4666

Since the late 1960s, the Educational Activities Early Childhood Catalog has offered an in-depth selection of musical recordings for classroom use which focus on the development of early-childhood motor and perceptual skills, language and math skills, patriotic and holiday songs, and square-dance music. In addition to classroom-oriented books, computer software, videotapes, and filmstrips, this catalog now lists an enticing selection of superb yet hard-to-find recordings that parents will want to enjoy with their children at home. Important recordings by Hap Palmer, Rick Charette, Ella Jenkins, Marcia Berman, and Patty Zeitlin are all available here.

Kimbo Educational

P.O. Box 477E

Long Branch, NJ 07740

(201) 229-4949

Geared for early childhood classroom use, the Kimbo Educational catalog offers parents many titles that they will enjoy sharing with their children at home. While Kimbo lists recordings in a variety of areas, it has an especially strong focus on fitness for kids.

Beginning with youngest listeners, Kimbo has produced an impressive list of their own activity recordings, including *Diaper Gym, Touch, Teach and Hug a Toddler, Baby Games, Bean Bag Fun,* and the award-winning *Toddlers on Parade.* For preschoolers and early-elementary children, Kimbo offers titles dealing with aerobics, rhythm bands, square dancing, feelings and emotions, self-help skills, and science information, including Jane Murphy's *Once Upon a Dinosaur* and Slim Goodbody's *Musical Guide to What's Inside.*

Ladyslipper

P.O. Box 3130

Durham, NC 27705

(919) 683-1570

Ladyslipper is a nonprofit organization which has been involved in many facets of women's music since 1976. If you are an adventurous, worldly music listener, this catalog is one to have. Filling more than seventy-five pages with listings of music by women artists, divided by style and content, titles are annotated with helpful comments. In addition to six pages of top-notch recordings for children, Ladyslipper offers a sophisticated collection of recordings by women who create rich music for adult listening.

Linden Tree

170 State St.

Los Altos, CA 94022

(415) 949-3390

While the least elegant visually (it's a staple-bound computer printout), the Linden Tree catalog, with more than fourteen hundred titles, is a great resource for wonderful yet nearly impossible-to-find recordings. Linden Tree now has expanded

to include Linden International in Issaquah, Washington. Customers at both locations are encouraged to listen to recordings *before* they make purchases—what
an innovation!

Music for Little People

P.O. Box 1460
Redway, CA 95560
(800) 836-4445

More than twenty colorful pages of musical offerings, lovingly annotated and
exquisitely adorned with woodland elves, animals, and children, make Music for
Little People the shining star of catalogs. You must see it!

Focused primarily on child-oriented audio and video recording and instruments,
Music for Little People also offers a small sampling of carefully selected books and
listening accessories. For new listeners, Music for Little People has assembled
several modestly priced sampler tapes and now offers a song-line service which
allows customers with touch-tone phones to hear thirty seconds of a selection
from any of the cassette tapes in the catalog.

Upbeat

163 Joralemon St., Suite 1250
Brooklyn, NY 11201
(718) 522-5349

You'll get individualized help when placing an order from the attractive, selective
Upbeat catalog, which specializes in quality audio and video tapes for children. If
you want a recording that you don't see listed, they will do their best to find it
for you.

Wireless

Minnesota Public Radio
274 Fillmore Ave. East
St. Paul, MN 55107
(800) 328-5252

While it's certainly not a "children's catalog," I couldn't resist including Wireless
because of its commitment to good music. A gift catalog issued by Minnesota Public
Radio, Wireless offers an inspired potpourri of recordings perfect for family listening. With recordings of Garrison Keillor's humorous and musical radio program

"Prairie Home Companion" as its mainstay, Wireless carries an ever-changing, worthwhile selection of music, which has included American folk music, classical music, fifties hits by the original artists, New Age music, and music from the British Isles. In addition, you'll find a delightful assortment of radio classics, music listening paraphernalia, and music-oriented T-shirts.

The All Ears Sampler of Music: The Artists and Their Recordings

When I first proposed *All Ears* to my publisher four years ago, I had the ambitious idea that I would be able to include every recording available for family listening. Halfway through its assembly I realized my folly. One glance through any of the major music catalogs will reveal just how many recordings are now available for family listening. The field of music for family listening has grown faster than I, as one person, could document. With regret and frustration I have had to accept that *All Ears* would not be a definitive encyclopedia of children's music.

On the other hand, the emergence of so many high-caliber recordings has reaffirmed the importance of my message. After several years of searching and listening, my overall purpose in writing *All Ears* remains enthusiastically the same:

- to excite adults about the value of intergenerational listening by outlining the benefits for children from birth to age ten.
- to define the strengths and qualities of the newly blossoming field of family listening. Once considered a dumping ground for artists who "just couldn't make it" in the adult world, the children's music industry is now dominated by innovative and gifted musicians, songwriters, and producers whose goals are to make sensitive, positive contributions to the quality of family life.
- to describe recordings for family listening so that adults can make educated

and successful selections when purchasing recordings for their family or group of children.

Who and What Are in the All Ears Sampler

Included in the Sampler are profiles of artists and overviews of specific recordings that I feel have made significant and innovative contributions to the contemporary field of music for family listening. Each recording upholds and enhances a musical tradition or combines an eclectic musical sound with literate, child-oriented lyrics that encourage one or more of the following qualities:

- independent and creative thinking
- appreciation of diversity and self-determination
- acknowledgment of our changing world
- concern for harmony in the family, the community, and the world
- respect for learning through rhythm, movement, fantasy, and humor.

Overall, the musical recordings that appear in the Sampler promote singing, moving, sensing, thinking, caring, sharing, and growth for listeners of all ages.

The Selection Process

The recordings listed in the Sampler hold up well and often blossom with repeated exposure. I know—I have listened to every recording included here many times. In fact, in the course of my total immersion, I became deeply involved with many of them.

In addition to listening to hundreds of recordings hundreds of times myself, I shared recordings with many wonderful children and adults. By lending records and cassettes to both parent and teacher friends, giving recordings as baby and birthday gifts, and helping people select recordings at the East Woods School Book Fair, I was able to instigate a lot of family and group listening. In all cases, I asked both adults and children to report back to me.

My own son, Jesse, was, of course, an important listening barometer, as was every one of his friends who wandered through our house or rode for more than five minutes in our car. I was especially gratified when a child would get in my car and ask to hear a specific song or album that I had played during a previous ride.

The Recording Artists

While most of the artists who have made recordings for children began their careers performing for adults, many (including Raffi, ROSENSHONTZ, Sharon, Lois and Bram, and Frank Cappelli) have shifted their focus because they discovered that their true talent lay in communicating with family audiences. Others (Tom Paxton, John McCutcheon, Cathy Fink, Marcy Marxer, Lois LaFond, and Jon Crosse) have taken time from their careers as performers for adults to create recordings for young listeners, often as an outgrowth of being parents themselves.

Many of the seventy artists I have described in *All Ears* have received awards for their recordings from either or both the American Library Association and Parents' Choice, two important pro-child organizations. Other artists I have included because I feel that they too are making significant contributions to the field of music for family listening.

But there may be twice as many people whose work is deserving of recognition who have been left out because of limitations of time and space. To artists and readers alike, I extend my apologies for these omissions. While I look forward to doubling the list in a future edition of *All Ears,* I also hope that this first edition will inspire readers to seek out the additional channels I have suggested so that they can continue to identify what is rewarding and enjoyable for their listeners.

Finally, I urge adults to share their enthusiasm for their favorite recordings with others, and to learn about new recordings by talking to teachers, librarians, parents, and shop owners. Seek out radio shows for children, as well as catalogs, media reviews, and parenting publications. Above all, listen with children and pay attention to what they like to hear!

Using the Listings

Browse through the selections that follow at your leisure with an eye toward recordings that are age and theme appropriate for your family. Personal preferences, timing, and age appropriateness will all be key factors in what your family will grow to cherish, so be sure to read chapter 5, which clarifies these issues.

Index by Age Appropriateness

If a name appears in the list below under several age categories, it indicates that the artist or group has created a number of recordings that are targeted differently. Be sure to choose the recording appropriate to your needs.

Theme and Topic Index

The artists named below, all profiled in the Sampler section that follows, have created recordings with predominating themes and topics. Many artists have devoted entire albums to a particular theme; those with asterisks before their names include a few songs with that theme in their albums. While this list is far from complete, it is offered as an aid for parents and teachers in selecting material appropriate for sharing with their children. For more specific information, see the biographical descriptions.

Abilities and Disabilities
The Kids of Widney High
Kids on the Block
*Tickle Tune Typhoon
*Uncle Ruthie

Activities for
Infants and Toddlers
John Feierabend
Tom Glazer
Bob McGrath and Katharine Smithrim

Activities for Preschoolers
Marcia Berman
Rachel Buchman
Janice Buckner
Tom Glazer
Ella Jenkins
Bob McGrath
Marcy Marxer
Paul Strausman
Uncle Ruthie

Animals
*Heather Bishop
*Janice Buckner
*Frank Cappelli
Francine Lancaster
Mary Miché
*Tom Paxton
David Polansky
*Barry Louis Polisar
*Raffi
*ROSENSHONTZ
Phil Rosenthal

Kevin Roth
Pete Seeger
*Sharon, Lois and Bram
Paul Strausman

Caring and Sharing
Marcia Berman
The Children of Selma
*Cathy Fink
*Gary Lapow
*Raffi
ROSENSHONTZ
*Jim Valley

Dinosaurs
*Mary Miché
*Barry Louis Polisar
*Paul Strausman
*Tickle Tune Typhoon
Michele Valeri and Michael Stein

Dolphins and Whales
*John McCutcheon
*Sarah Pirtle
*Raffi
*Nancy Silber and Tony Soll
*Jim Valley
*The Weavers

Family, Friendship, and
Contemporary Life-Styles
*Peter Alsop
*Heather Bishop
*Kim and Jerry Brodey
*Janice Buckner

*Tom Chapin
*Rick Charette
*Charlotte Diamond
*Bill Harley
*John McCutcheon
*Eric Nagler
*Hap Palmer
*Barry Louis Polisar
*ROSENSHONTZ
Marlo Thomas and Friends
*Uncle Ruthie

Food, Health, and Fitness
*Peter Alsop
Janet and Judy
*David Polansky
*Barry Louis Polisar
*ROSENSHONTZ
*Tickle Tune Typhoon
*"Weird Al" Yankovic

Freedom and Peace
*Peter Alsop
*Linda Arnold
*Kim and Jerry Brodey
The Children of Selma
*Charlotte Diamond
Red Grammer
*Bill Harley
Mary Miché
Sally Rogers
Sweet Honey in the Rock

Holidays
Fran Avni
Francine Lancaster
Mary Miché

Raffi
Tickle Tune Typhoon

Imagination
Peter Alsop
Linda Arnold
Kim and Jerry Brodey
Frank Cappelli
Tom Chapin
Rick Charette
Charlotte Diamond
Bill Harley
Chris Holder
Eric Nagler
Tim Noah
Hap Palmer
Barry Louis Polisar
ROSENSHONTZ
Paul Tracey
Jim Valley

Language Arts
Janet and Judy

Lullabies and Nursery Rhymes
Pamala Ballingham
Joanie Bartels
Steve Bergman
Pat Carfra
Jon Crosse
*Jonathan Edwards
Terrence Farrell
*Kathi and Milenko, Nancy Rumbel, and
   Friends
Lois LaFond
Francine Lancaster
Kevin Roth

Sharon, Lois and Bram
Stephen Tosh

Monsters and Fear
Charlotte Diamond
*Bill Harley
*Barry Louis Polisar
*Tickle Tune Typhoon
*Troubadour

Personal Welfare
Peter Alsop
Rick Charette
Tickle Tune Typhoon

School
*Tom Chapin
*Bill Harley
*David Polansky
*Barry Louis Polisar

Science, Nature, and Ecology
Marcia Berman and Patty Zeitlin
*Tom Chapin
Janet and Judy
*John McCutcheon
Mary Miché
*Sarah Pirtle
*Tickle Tune Typhoon

Self-Esteem
Peter Alsop
Lisa Atkinson
Marcia Berman and Patty Zeitlin
Janice Buckner
*Howard Hanger
The Kids of Widney High

Kids on the Block
Lois LaFond
Hap Palmer
Barry Louis Polisar
ROSENSHONTZ
Nancy Silber and Tony Soll
Marlo Thomas and Friends
Tickle Tune Typhoon
Troubadour
Uncle Ruthie
Jim Valley

Traditional and International Songs
Marcia Berman
*Rachel Buchman
*Charlotte Diamond
*Jonathan Edwards
Gemini
*Bill Harley
Chris Holder
Ella Jenkins
Lois LaFond
Raffi
Phil Rosenthal
Pete Seeger
Sharon, Lois and Bram
Tickle Tune Typhoon
Bill Usher
The Weavers

Transportation
*Janice Buckner
*Frank Cappelli
*Tom Glazer
Chris Holder

The All Ears Sampler

Peter Alsop

With a Ph.D. in educational psychology, singer, humorist, and humanist Peter Alsop creates songs that are used by thousands of parents, educators, and human-service professionals to help families discuss sensitive issues. Combining his backgrounds in education, music, and theater, Peter has produced and recorded ten recordings, some aimed at adults, some geared for children. "I don't consider this kids' stuff," Alsop has said of his recordings for younger listeners. "I consider this family stuff."

The songs on Peter Alsop's family albums are often funny and profound as they encourage independent thinking and frank discussion. "Adults who get the most from these songs are those who participate in the silliness with their children," says Alsop. Ideas for exercises, questions, and discussion topics are included as well as lyrics.

To receive a catalog of Peter Alsop's work—recordings, songbooks, and film strips—as well as for booking information, write to Peter Alsop, P.O. Box 960, Topanga, California 90290.

Wha'Da'Ya'Wanna Do? (1983)
Flying Fish Records
1304 W. Schubert
Chicago, IL 60614

Format: Cassette, LP
Age Appeal: 5 and up
Target Ages: 5–8
Material: Songs that deal with contemporary issues of childhood, including bore-dom, creativity, siblings, being gross, death, and our right to privacy for our bodies
Vocals: Peter Alsop and children
Vocal Style: Contemporary folk
Instrumentation: Guitars, piano, drums, dulcimer, harmonica, wooden spoons, concertina, jaw harp

Wha'Da'Ya'Wanna Do? addresses many contemporary issues for children with imaginative, humorous images. The songs are strung together with a playful nar-rative by Alsop and a group of neighborhood children who drop by to play and sing, and are written and performed primarily from a child's point of view. Alsop has an informal, friendly manner that enables him to discuss topics that have long been considered taboo: for example, he clearly distinguishes between a secret that is a nice surprise and one that is hurtful and destructive.

Highlights include "Bored, Bored, Bored," every kid's complaint; "Wha'Da'Ya'Wanna Do?," promoting creative messes; "My Brother Threw Up on My Stuffed Toy Bunny," the Polisar classic; "Yecch," a scream-along song about the fun of being grossed out; "I Am a Pizza," Alsop's delicious masterpiece about pretending; "No One Knows for Sure," a bittersweet yet optimistic song that asks us to do the best we can even though no one can predict the twists and turns of life; "My Body," a popular request on radio's "Kids America," a credo sung by kids about their right to be the stewards of their own bodies; "You Get a Little Extra When You Watch TV," about the specific messages given off by TV—if *All Ears* had a theme song, this would be it.

Take Me with You (1986)

Moose School Records
P.O. Box 960
Topanga, CA 90290
Format: Cassette, LP
Age Appeal: 3 and up
Target Ages: 3–10

Material: Songs that deal with contemporary issues of childhood, including seatbelt safety, peace, overcoming failure, sexual abuse, and parental expectations

Using a car ride as the unifying element, the title song, "Take Me with You," lists compelling reasons not to leave a child behind. Additional highlights include "Irish Seat Belt Jig," reinforcing the importance of using seat belts; "Gnarly Dude," about a kid who has learned that sometimes it pays to study his teacher rather than study the subject; "Hey, Ev'rybody," about the joys of mastering something; "It's No Fun When Ya Gotta Eat an Onion," about different tastes; "Chickens for Peace," a rousing, humorous, effective anthem complete with clucks and bucks; "The Letter to Mr. Brown," about kids' needs to be touched appropriately; "He Eats Asparagus, Why Can't You Be That Way?," Barry Louis Polisar's song about parental expectations; "Logical," enumerating the universal arguments between parents and children about eating dessert, being too sick for school, overcoming fears, and the necessity of taking a bath; and "Kids' Peace Song," a calypso tune about the diversity of people on the outside and the similarities of people on the inside.

Stayin' Over (1987)
Moose School Records
Format: Cassette, LP
Age Appeal: 3–12
Target Ages: 8–10
Material: Songs that address sensitive issues for contemporary children, including dealing with human imperfection, divorce, death, and alcohol

Peter Alsop knows that while adults and children often need to talk together about serious issues, sometimes it's difficult for them to find safe, comfortable ways to communicate. To open up important interaction, he has created *Stayin' Over.*

A sleep-over at Peter's house is the occasion for fun, soul searching, and communication. Song highlights include the title song; "Bigger, Bigger, Bigger," about adults who treat children as if might makes right; "I Wanna Try It," a plea for kids' rights to have hands-on learning experiences (adults can't seem to stand back and give their kids a chance to learn by doing); "Dear Mr. President," about how kids collecting stickers find that their need to outdo each other results in violence; "Us Kids Brush Our Teeth," about respecting personal methods; "If You Love a Hippopotamus," which says if someone is your friend it doesn't matter what she looks like.

Linda Arnold

In response to a request by her daughter, Katie, to hear a song about "a short giraffe on a crooked path," silvery-voiced Linda Arnold wrote "Do You Know What Magic Is?" And so began a career of writing and performing songs that celebrate the joys of fantasy and childhood.

Frequent performances around her home area of Santa Cruz, California, have expanded into national projects, increasing Linda's visibility in a big way. In addition to hosting the syndicated, award-winning radio show "Pickleberry Pie," Linda is reaching a huge new audience on cable TV through a forty-five-minute concert video aired on the Disney Channel. Her audio cassettes are now being distributed across the country by music-industry giant A&M Records.

At this writing, Linda has produced two recordings with a refreshing, contemporary sound. Katie, whose remarkable singing voice is maturing in front of our ears, has become a frequent recording partner, and Linda's young son, Toby, is beginning to get into the act.

Make Believe (1986)

Ariel Records
P.O. Box 2999
Santa Cruz, CA 95062
Distributed by A&M Records
1416 N. LaBrea Ave.
Hollywood, CA 90028
Format: Cassette
Target Ages: 3–7
Material: Songs that promote imagination and peaceful coexistence (All compositions are by Linda Arnold except where noted.)
Vocals: Linda Arnold with children's chorus and solos by Katie Thiermann, Linda's eight-year-old daughter
Vocal Style: Clear, sparkling pop soprano
Instrumentation: guitars, dulcimer, keyboards, flute, oboe, cello, banjo, Autoharp, percussion

Here's a winning recording that will make the whole family feel good. With songs that promote fantasy, spontaneity, and family life, *Make Believe* offers playful images and tunes.

Songs of special note include the graceful and memorable "Do You Know What Magic Is?," "Stone Soup," a jaunty song that makes it fun to concoct fantasy food; "Be Kind to Your Parents," a treasure to be enjoyed by parents and children, sung affectingly by young Katie; "Christmas Mouse," with its catchy tune and humorous story of overindulgence on candy which will strike a familiar note with many listeners.

Also by Linda Arnold is *Happiness Cake,* released in 1989 on A&M Records.

Lisa Atkinson

With a zesty singing voice that might be an amalgam of Ethel Merman, Maria Muldaur, and a sensitive, playful nursery-school teacher, Lisa Atkinson serves up recordings that will surprise and delight adult listeners as well as preschoolers. Her skillful blending of a sophisticated sound with an early-childhood sensibility will win her many fans.

I Wanna Tickle the Fish (1987)
A Gentle Wind
P.O. Box 3103
Albany, NY 12203
Format: Cassette
Target Ages: 2–5
Material: Engaging original songs of reassurance, acknowledging the concerns of preschoolers, promoting their self-determination and development of positive feelings
Vocals: Lisa Atkinson with backup vocals
Vocal Style: Zesty and tuneful
Instrumentation: Guitar, synthesizer, percussion, flute, harmonica, kazoo

Feisty yet sensitive, *I Wanna Tickle the Fish* contains songs that articulate what it feels like to be young, small, and growing.

In addition to the offbeat and memorable title song, of special note are "You Can Be a Giant," "Dandelions," and "Growing Song."

Fran Avni

Fran Avni and Jackie Cytrynbaum founded Lemonstone Records in 1980. At that time Avni, a Canadian-born composer and performer, had a well-established career in Israel. Cytrynbaum was an early-childhood educator and songwriter in Canada.

On their independent, Montreal-based label, they have created the three Jewish-culture recordings listed below as well as the secular *Artichokes and Brussels Sprouts.* Cytrynbaum's contemporary musical approach and Avni's expressive, resonant voice make this music perfect for strengthening intergenerational, as well as cross-cultural, understanding and appreciation.

Latkes and Hamentashen (1978)

Lemonstone Records
P.O. Box 607
Côte-St-Luc, Quebec, Canada H4V 2Z2
Format: Cassette, LP
Age Appeal: 4–7
Material: Narration and songs that describe the history and ritual surrounding the Jewish celebrations of Chanukah and Purim
Vocals: Fran Avni
Narration: Randy Lutterman
Vocal Style: Folk/pop
Instrumentation: Guitars, Autoharp, kazoo, drums, flute, recorders, keyboard, banjo, conga

Latkes and Hamentashen is a collection of upbeat contemporary songs about Jewish history and tradition, strung together with no-nonsense narration describing the historic struggles that became the basis for Jewish ritual. Telling the stories of Chanukah on side 1 and Purim on side 2, Fran Avni's pleasant singing voice is accompanied by jazz, blues, and bluegrass arrangements that, in a surprising break from tradition, open new doors to intergenerational and intercultural understanding, enjoyment, and respect. A preschool workbook is available to enrich the listening experience. Incorporating reading and math readiness, it is available through Lemonstone.

Mostly Matzah (1983)

Lemonstone Records

Format: Cassette, LP

Age Appeal: 5–9

Material: Traditional narration and contemporary songs that describe the history and ritual surrounding the Jewish celebration of Passover

Vocals: Fran Avni

Narration: Randy Lutterman

Vocal Style: Folk/pop

Instrumentation: Guitars, Autoharp, kazoo, drums, flute, recorders, keyboard, banjo, conga

Describing the Jewish celebration of Passover, *Mostly Matzah* is energetic and fresh. Most of the songs are new creations, and the old standbys are treated to updated interpretations. "Mah Nishtanah"—the four questions traditionally asked by the youngest boy at the Passover seder—is sung by Fran's two young daughters.

The Seventh Day (1984)

Lemonstone Records

Format: Cassette, LP

Age Appeal: 4–8

Material: Songs explaining the concept and practices of the Jewish Shabbat as well as songs that address more universal themes contained in the New Testament

Vocals: Fran Avni with children

Narration: Randy Lutterman

Vocal Style: Folk/pop

Instrumentation: Guitars, Autoharp, kazoo, drums, flute, recorders, keyboard, banjo, conga

While some of the songs are about the Jewish Shabbat, many on *The Seventh Day* are more universal in concept, with a large number about Old Testament themes. Breaking with the form established on Avni's first two recordings (see above), *The Seventh Day* flows from song to song without the structure of narration maintaining the strictly Jewish focus.

Pamala Ballingham

The song selections, Pamala Ballingham's reedy vocals, and the ethereal instrumentation blend together to create a faraway, dreamlike ambience. Each volume of this award-winning series is more than a hundred minutes long.

Earth Mother Lullabies from Around the World, Volume 1 (1984)

Earth Mother Productions, Inc.
P.O. Box 43204
Tucson, AZ 85733
Format: Cassette
Age Appeal: Newborn–3
Material: Lullabies from a variety of countries and cultures, intended to relax and nurture people of all ages
Vocals: Pamala Ballingham
Vocal Style: Clear soprano, occasionally reminiscent of Joan Baez
Instrumentation: Soothing music created by harp, flute, mandolin, guitar, percussion

Song highlights include "Arrorró, Mi Niño" from Latin America, "Sleep, My Baby" from Russia, "Sleep, Little One" from Japan, "Ushururu" from Ethiopia, "Ho Ho Watanay" from Iroquois, "Sleep, My Darling, Sleep" from Iceland, and "The Mockingbird Song" from Appalachia.

Earth Mother Lullabies from Around the World, Volume 2 (1987)

As above, except:
Instrumentation: Also includes Tibetan bell, sound effects, and keyboard

Highlights include "Tum-Balalayka" (Yiddish), "All the Pretty Little Horses" (Afro-American), "Little Red Bird" (Isle of Man), "O Mother Glasco" (Afro-American), "Gaelic Cradle Song" (Irish), and "Kishmul Cradle Croon" (Hebrides).

Joanie Bartels

Producer Ellen Wohlstadter of Discovery Music has assembled an innovative series of recordings on which vocalist Joanie Bartels combines traditional lullabies with gentle interpretations of contemporary compositions that previously have not been presented as lullabies or music for young children. Carefully researched productions, these recordings are now used in hospitals and medical centers to soothe pregnant women as well as to comfort and stimulate newborns and nurses.

Other titles in this series include *Morning Magic, Lullaby Magic II, Travelin' Magic,* and *Silly Time Magic.*

Lullaby Magic (1985)

Discovery Music
4130 Greenbush Avenue
Sherman Oaks, CA 91423
Format: Cassette
Age Appeal: Newborn–4
Material: Traditional and contemporary lullabies
Vocals: Joanie Bartels
Vocal Style: Sweet, smoky soprano with eclectic sound including folk-rock and pop
Instrumentation: Piano, strings, oboe, bassoon, percussion

Selections include "Close Your Eyes," "Golden Slumbers," "Rock-a-Bye Baby," "Wynken, Blynken and Nod," "All the Pretty Little Horses," "Hush Little Baby," "Goodnight, My Someone," "Twinkle, Twinkle," and "Lullaby and Goodnight." Side 2 contains instrumental renditions of the same material.

Steve Bergman

Having produced more than two dozen titles, musician Steve Bergman is making a life's career of creating music to help people relax. From unborn infants to stressed-out executives, "most of us benefit from and love music that calms us, nurtures us, inspires us," says Bergman.

Of special note to parents of infants and toddlers are three instrumental recordings. *Sweet Baby Dreams,* containing music interwoven with the heartbeat of pregnant women, is geared to creating a comforting atmosphere for crying babies. *Slumberland* is a collection of quieting tunes meant to be helpful before naps and bedtime. *Lullabies from Around the World* contains orchestral interpretations of traditional lullabies, incorporating a mother's heartbeat and nature sounds.

Lullabies from Around the World (1983)

Steve Bergman
P.O. Box 4577
Carmel, CA 93921
Format: Cassette
Age Appeal: Newborn–4
Material: Traditional lullabies with an ethereal sound
Vocals: None
Instrumentation: Flute, guitar, keyboards, synthesizer, sound effects

Selections include "Rockaby Baby" (Canada), "Soli, Soli, Dittali" (Switzerland), "Arrorró, Mi Niño" (South America), "Gartan Mother's Lullaby" (Ireland), and "Hush, Little Baby" (United States).

Marcia Berman, Patty Zeitlin, Anne Lief Barlin

Marcia Berman's elegant, clear voice is perfect for sending positive musical messages to young listeners. Always warm and melodic, never preachy or forced, Marcia creates age-appropriate yet quietly sophisticated songs that speak directly to children's emotions, helping them to understand and articulate their feelings.

A veteran of the children's music scene, Los Angeles–based Berman has been a singer, songwriter, and teacher of children for more than thirty years. Working alone and with collaborators Patty Zeitlin and Anne Lief Barlin, she has produced and performed on ten recordings, many of which are established mainstays in preschool classrooms. While the Berman-Barlin-Zeitlin recordings have been well known by classroom teachers for years, these exquisite recordings are equally appropriate for family listening.

Marcia Berman Sings Malvina Reynolds'
"Rabbits Dance" and Other Songs for Children (1985)

B/B Records
570 N. Arden Blvd.
Los Angeles, CA 90004
Format: Cassette, LP
Age appeal: 18 months–3 years

Vocals: Marcia Berman and C.A.M.A.L. Chorus: Peter Alsop, Uncle Ruthie, Dan Crow, Miriam Cutler, J. P. Nightingale, Mallory Pearce, Patty Zeitlin
Vocal Style: Clear, melodious, folk based
Instrumentation: Guitar, piano, synthesizer, percussion, clarinet, shakuhachi

Caring and sharing is the overall theme of *Marcia Berman Sings Malvina Reynolds' "Rabbits Dance."* Malvina Reynolds, who died in 1978, wrote innovative, humanistic songs for children. Marcia Berman's warm interpretations are enhanced with simple but rich accompaniments that add an elegant touch to these contemporary masterpieces. Gentle in sound yet sophisticated in content, this is an album for parents and preschoolers to listen to many times so that they can enjoy the benefits of having its messages and music become part of their lives together. Lyrics are included.

Highlights of this rich recording include "I Live in a City," a celebration of humanity that invites listeners to clap along and rejoice about people working together; the particularly timely "Place to Be," which emphasizes that just as birds and fish have their own places in the world, people need places of their own as well; "You Can't Make Turtle Come Out," which explains that while shy creatures are easily overwhelmed, once left alone they become more willing to deal with the world; "Jenny Fell Down," which helps preschoolers pick themselves up and get on with their day; "Morningtown Ride," a lilting lullaby which should figure importantly in the family repertoire of goodnight songs (parents of preschool-age train aficionados should be sure to bring it to their child's attention); and "Magic Penny," Malvina Reynolds's optimistic, upbeat masterpiece about the value of sharing.

Spin, Spider, Spin (1973)
Educational Activities, Inc.
P.O. Box 392
Freeport, NY 11520
Format: Cassette, LP
Age Appeal: 2–4
Material: Songs about nature by Patty Zeitlin and Marcia Berman
Vocals: Patty Zeitlin, Marcia Berman, Dave Zeitlin
Vocal Style: Contemporary folk
Instrumentation: Guitars, harmonica, flute

A poetic celebration of nature and animal life, *Spin, Spider, Spin* contains delightful, intelligent songs about spiders, lizards, birds, worms, and snails. With lovely vocals and gentle instrumentation, *Spin, Spider, Spin* is a perfect vehicle for enhancing preschoolers' natural fascination for crawling creatures and the environment.

Song highlights include "I Love Lizards," "Just a Snail," "Lots of Worms," "The Way of the Bees," "Down by the Creek," "Night Sounds," and "Frogs' and Crickets' Lullaby."

Everybody Cries Sometimes (1971)

Educational Activities, Inc.

Format: Cassette, LP

Age Appeal: 2–4

Material: Songs to help children gain confidence by learning to appreciate themselves and others, with material written by Patty Zeitlin, Marcia Berman, Malvina Reynolds, and Woody Guthrie; also includes lyric and activity book for teachers and parents

Vocals: Marcia Berman and Patty Zeitlin

Vocal Style: Ragtime, blues, and gospel influence

Instrumentation: Guitar by Dave Zeitlin and piano by John Bucchino

While the title may lead you to assume this is an album of maudlin songs for children, nothing could be farther from the truth. Available with a fine teachers' guide, this is a poetic, upbeat collection of activity songs for preschoolers that parents can enjoy sharing with their children at home. As described on the album cover, these are "songs for self-appreciation and self-expression."

Highlights include "Beautiful Arms," a dance tune with a tinkly ragtime piano accompaniment to encourage children to celebrate what they can do with their arms; "One Little Bird," a finger-play song that demonstrates volume and growth through the addition of each child's voice; "Here's a Song," which promotes the importance of observation and eye contact (giving each child in the group the pleasure of being the center of attention, if only for a few moments, it can be equally effective sung in the classroom or in a family group); "Room in the Boat," a simple tune about belonging performed with a gospel sound (a zipper song, it allows parents and teachers to personalize the singing experience by substituting the names of each child in their group); and "Everybody Cries Sometimes," which helps children appreciate that crying has a meaningful place in their lives (sung by Dave Zeitlin, this songs tells children, boys especially, that crying is one way that human beings can heal their emotional hurts).

Dance-a-Story, Sing-a-Song (1980)
B/B Records
570 N. Arden Blvd.
Los Angeles, CA 90004
Format: Cassette, LP
Age Appeal: 2–4
Material: Activity songs and stories from around the world, including Africa, Japan, Holland, Mexico, Israel, and the Ozark Mountains, adapted by Marcia Berman and Anne Lief Barlin
Vocals: Marcia Berman and others
Vocal Style: Musical narrative
Instrumentation: Piano, guitar, bassoon, accordion, recorder, dulcimer, African slit drum, glockenspiel, xylophone, metallophone

Dance-a-Story, Sing-a-Song contains carefully crafted musical stories and songs from many cultures. "The Wooden Doll," on side 1, is an imaginative tale about a doll who changes piece by piece from wooden parts to raggedy parts. By listening and participating, preschoolers are encouraged "to locate, isolate, and articulate all of the body parts."

Highlights of side 2 include "Oh, John the Rabbit," an Afro-American call-and-response song about what grows in the garden; "Shojoji," a Japanese song about badgers who dance in the moonlight in the garden of the beautiful Shojoji Temple; "Die Klokken," Dutch, about the tick-tocking of the clock; and "Homentashin," a tale about the Jewish holiday of Purim.

Heather Bishop

Bellybutton (1982)
Mother of Pearl Records, Inc.
Woodmore, Manitoba, Canada R0A 2M0
Format: Cassette
Age Appeal: All ages
Target Ages: 5–8

Material: Original songs of fantasy, humanity, and friendship, mostly written by Connie Caldor; lyrics included
Vocals: Heather Bishop with backup
Vocal Style: Powerful blues/pop/rock
Instrumentation: Guitars, piano, synthesizer, percussion, fiddle, tuba

Bellybutton is a unique and satisfying recording featuring the tart and bluesy singing of Heather Bishop. Her expressive delivery, the offbeat, humorous songs, and the imaginative backups combine to create rich listening that will intrigue worldly children and adults.

Highlights include Bishop's slithery rendition of "The Alligator Waltz" and her comic delivery of "If You Love a Hippopotamus."

Also by Heather Bishop on Mother of Pearl Records: *Purple People Eater* (1984).

Kim and Jerry Brodey

The recordings of Kim and Jerry Brodey contain a blend of traditional songs and contemporary compositions which deal with issues of ecology, global friendship, cross-cultural awareness, technology, and contemporary families. In addition to its content, the Brodeys' music has a sparkling, up-to-the-minute ambience that can stand up to commercial television and radio for your family's attention. In fact, the Brodeys' sound is so exuberant and full, it is the perfect choice for families with early-elementary-age children who, so smitten with the sounds of Top 40 music, have little interest in anything else. Both children and adults will find it hard to resist dancing when Kim and Jerry Brodey's music fills the airwaves.

Jerry, a former teacher, is the songwriter and musician of the duo. Kim, a trained mime, has a powerful voice which blends impressively with Jerry's. This dynamic duo spends much of its time touring North America giving energetic, theatrical school and family performances that encourage audiences of all ages to think and use their imaginations as they have the time of their lives.

Simple Magic (1984)
The Children's Group
The Children's Book Store Distribution
561 Bloor St. West, Suite 300
Toronto, Ontario, Canada M5S 1Y6

Format: Cassette, LP
Age Appeal: 4–9
Material: Contemporary issues and traditional songs with upbeat, high-energy interpretations
Vocals: Kim and Jerry Brodey and children's chorus
Vocal style: Soaring, full rock sound with elegant harmonies
Instrumentation: Guitar, banjo, mandolin, synthesizer, saxophone, violin

The Brodeys weave their musical magic to create contemporary sounds that will appeal to even the most media-saturated children. While many of the songs are traditional, the treatment is so rich they sound like they are the best of the Top Ten chart. The original songs are written by Jerry Brodey. Highlights include "The Captain and Me," a touching song about meeting a whale in a dream; "There Is a Robot," about getting to know a computerized stranger in outer space; and "I'm Going to Toronto," a rock 'n' roll version of the traditional "Shake It Like a Milkshake."

Family Pie (1986)

The Children's Group
Format: Cassette, LP
Age Appeal: All ages
Target Ages: 5–10
Material: Contemporary family life depicted with spirit and openmindedness. The main issue here is learning to accept the blended family.
Vocals: Kim and Jerry Brodey, their sons, Joshua and Oliver, and children's chorus
Vocal Style: High-energy, contemporary sound, highlighted by rich harmonies and some energetic belting from Kim
Instrumentation: Guitar, banjo, mandolin, synthesizer, saxophone

Family Pie is a collection of mostly original songs that ring with energy and truth. The first song, "Let's Help This Planet," serves up a full, rock sound as it asks us to be ecologically and interpersonally responsible. "This Is My Family" is an upbeat but tell-it-like-it-is song that describes the Brodeys' own extended family. In it, the Brodeys' sons, Josh and Oliver, sing affectingly about how they have adapted to their new family configurations. In "Masked Bandits," a personal favorite of mine, the Brodeys tell a humorous tale about raccoons invading their family campsite. Encouraging listeners' imagination, "I've Gone Inside My TV" exuberantly asks,

"Is life really like my TV set?" "Walking to Freedom," sung hauntingly by children, exudes the determination to overcome the shackles of slavery. And "A Simple Thing" is about the joys of being together as a family.

Rachel Buchman

A teacher and performer in the Boston area at schools where many preschoolers come from diverse cultural backgrounds, Rachel Buchman created her albums to help children learn English as well as to encourage them to share their heritage with others.

Hello Everybody! (1986)
A Gentle Wind
P.O. Box 3103
Albany, NY 12203
Format: Cassette
Target Ages: 1–3
Material: Original and traditional play songs and rhymes that reflect a toddler's world
Vocals: Rachel Buchman
Vocal Style: Intimate, unpretentious, and spirited folk style
Instrumentation: Guitar

Listening to *Hello Everybody!* is like having your child's favorite nursery-school teacher sitting on your living-room floor. Taking her inspiration from the approach developed by Charity Bailey back in the 1950s, Rachel Buchman has created a collection of singable songs that describe with reverence and delight the very simplest sensations, desires, fantasies, and experiences of toddlers. The spirited, ingenuous quality of this multi-award-winning recording will have parents and toddlers sharing the songs and activities long after Rachel has finished singing.

Rachel Buchman has also created *Hello Rachel! Hello Children!: Songs and Singing Games from the U.S. and Around the World,* on Rounder Records.

Janice Buckner

There's a special warmth that emanates from Janice Buckner and her music. Certified to teach elementary school as well as secondary English and social studies, Janice is the perfect example of today's high-caliber performer who combines her education and her musical talents with a genuine reverence for childhood and humanity. Her clear, tuneful voice and gentle humor inspire and excite the children who hear her perform. Several days after an assembly performance at East Woods School, many children dragged their parents to the music section of the school book fair specifically to purchase Janice Buckner recordings.

Janice's career is filled with appearances in community centers, schools, festivals, and libraries. Performances range from concerts to classroom workshops on puppetry, playwriting, songwriting, and sign language. With her husband, Dr. Richard Statler, who performs as the mime Rainyday Sunshine, she gives song, sign, and mime workshops. Janice is also a member, with Anna Epstein-Kravis, of the duo Sweet Rose Revue.

Little Friends for Little Folks (1986)
A Gentle Wind
Format: Cassette
Age Appeal: 2–5
Material: Original, singable activity and fantasy songs; songbook and activity guide available
Vocals: Janice Buckner with backup
Vocal Style: Warm and melodious, folk influenced
Instrumentation: Guitar, banjo, drums, percussion, synthesizer, silly noises

Janice Buckner has written a delightful assortment of singable songs that reinforce early learning skills. Liberally sprinkled with inviting sounds and phrases to repeat and imitate, *Little Friends for Little Folks* is great fun for young listeners and their families. Highlights include "The Train Song" and the humorous, exotic "Orangatango."

Everybody's Special (1988)
Moonlight Rose Publications
P.O. Box 154
Huntington, NY 11743

Format: Cassette
Age Appeal: All ages
Target Ages: 4–8
Material: Original songs celebrating life, promoting self-esteem and appreciation of others; songbook and activity guide available
Vocals: Janice Buckner
Vocal Style: Gentle, melodious, pop influenced
Instrumentation: Guitar, synthesizer

A cheerful, gentle recording, *Everybody's Special* is filled with upbeat songs that highlight affection, family, friendship, imagination, cooperation, differences in ability, self-reliance, and communication through sign language.

Highlights include "I Can Be Somebody," "Camille the Kissing Camel," "My Special Friends and Me," "Rockaby with Grandma," "Boogie Woogie Baby Boogie," "It's Great to Be Different," "I Can Talk with My Hands," and "Every Single Person Makes the World Go Round."

Frank Cappelli

Formerly the proprietors of a successful business in which Frank wrote and delivered wholesome singing telegrams, Frank and Patricia Cappelli knew it was time to move on when bawdy competitors began to emerge around them. Combining Frank's performing and writing talents, his degree in music education, and their love of children (the Cappellis have three young ones of their own), Frank and Patricia created the Peanut Heaven label. Utilizing Frank's strong, clear voice, which is softened to perfection by his friendly, warm personality, Peanut Heaven recordings offer music for little people delightfully served up with "big-people" sound.

His playful charm and timely mission—to help children experience the fun of learning through music—has led Frank Cappelli to become the host of "Cappelli and Company," a popular Pittsburgh-based television show for young children. In addition, all Frank Cappelli titles are now distributed by A&M Records, making them widely available across the country.

Beyond those described below, titles include *Look Both Ways* and *Good.*

You Wanna Be a Duck? (1987)

Peanut Heaven
717 N. Meadowcroft Ave.
Pittsburgh, PA 15216
Distributed by A&M Records
1416 N. LaBrea Ave.
Hollywood, CA 90028
Format: Cassette
Age Appeal: 2–5
Material: Humorous and gentle original songs by Frank Cappelli plus two old favorites
Vocals: Frank Cappelli, Gary Hohman, and the North Star Kids
Vocal Style: Clear, lilting tenor
Instrumentation: Guitars, banjo, Latin percussion, tambourine, violins, accordions, trumpet, trombones

Creating material that is gentle in attitude yet strong on flavor and wit, Frank Cappelli has assembled a roster of songs that are appropriate for preschool listeners. While far from Raffi clones, Frank Cappelli's recordings may be just the right choice for families who are baffled by whom to listen to next.

In addition to the humorous title song, "You Wanna Be a Duck?," which describes how to attain that rarefied state, highlights include "Yellow Truck," a long-needed love song that will have special meaning for truck-toting preschoolers; "Making a Pizza," in which Frank punches his voice up to an operatic range, giving special dignity and humor to the process of pizza making; and "The Fruit Market," a spirited add-on sing-along about shopping for fruit that will entice children into stretching their memories as they join in.

"The Swan Song," my runaway favorite of the recording, is a delightful introduction to the concepts of musical structure and sound. Frank reveals himself as a warm and charismatic narrator as he interacts with his friend Oliver the squirrel to define quarter notes, half notes, and eighth notes. With the clarinet, the cello, and the flute representing, respectively, ducks, a swan, and chicks, all the elements of the song come together so engagingly, listeners will wish that this delightful round would last longer. It's been thoughtfully placed at the end of the tape, where it's easy to rewind.

On Vacation (1987)

Peanut Heaven

Format: Cassette

Age Appeal: 3–5

Material: Informative original songs by Frank Cappelli that describe subjects including the jungle, golf, and the sounds of instruments

Vocals: Frank Cappelli and others

Vocal Style: Clear, direct, deceptively sophisticated sound

Instrumentation: Guitars, drums, marimba, conga, steel drum, mandolin, harmonica, fiddle, calliope, accordion, effects

Frank Cappelli uses a variety of upbeat musical styles, including reggae and country and western, to enhance his crystalline voice. Optimistic and filled with interesting information, the songs include "In the Jungle," which describes the habits and abilities of elephants, rhinos, and hippos; "Golf," an inventive introduction to the game that will finds fans among children whose parents play golf, or who have had fun playing miniature golf themselves; "Rat-a-Tat-Tat," a lovely introduction to the sounds made by instruments within the percussion, string, woodwind, and brass families; and "Oh, I Love the Clowns," in which Frank Cappelli celebrates his affection for the circus. (While many young children do adore the circus, others are frightened or intimidated by it. This song will be a good vehicle for helping listeners air their feelings.)

Pat Carfra

Known as "the Lullaby Lady," Pat Carfra creates recordings to encourage mothers and fathers to sing along with their children, a tradition she sees being threatened "as machines take over providing music for us."

Additional recordings by Pat Carfra include *Songs for Sleepy Heads and Out of Beds* and *Babes, Beasts and Birds.*

Lullabies and Laughter (1982)

Lullaby Lady Records

Distributed by A&M Records of Canada

939 Warden Ave.

Scarborough, Ontario, Canada M1L 4C5

Format: Cassette
Age Appeal: Newborn–3
Material: Traditional
Vocals: Pat Carfra
Vocal Style: Homey, clear, folk oriented
Instrumentation: Guitar, banjo, Autoharp

To encourage parents to sing to their babies, Pat Carfra offers specifics on how to personalize their singing for their own children. Side 1 contains lullabies; side 2, rhymes and play songs—thirty-three lullabies and play songs in all. Highlights include "Hush, Pretty Baby," "Morningtown Ride," "Jennifer's Rabbit," "Wynken, Blynken and Nod," "All the Pretty Little Horses," "Pop Goes the Weasel," "Eensy, Weensy Spider," "This Little Piggy," "Down by the Station," and "The Marvelous Toy."

Tom Chapin

Billboard magazine has called Tom Chapin "one of those natural-born entertainers who, with nothing more than a guitar in hand, can totally captivate an audience." This is no accident. Tom Chapin grew up in a musical family. Jim Chapin, his father, was a noted jazz drummer. Tom and his brothers, Harry and Steve, spent ten years performing together; they recorded their first album in 1965. When Harry left the act to pursue his own career, establishing himself as an innovative and remarkably successful story singer, Tom and Steve continued as a duo.

Focusing repeatedly on issues of humanity and the environment, Tom Chapin's career as an entertainer has grown in many directions over the years. Tom has now created two delightful recordings for family listening. With two young children of his own, he has tuned in to kids' needs and tastes. "And it's an enormous responsibility," he has said, "one that I can respond to as an entertainer by having as much fun as possible, being as interested as possible, providing positive music, and providing positive awareness about life and family relationships and our environment. . . . Maybe what I'm really doing is sharing—sharing the best of the kid in me and what the adult in me knows. It may be the most important work I've ever done. And the most rewarding."

Family Tree (1988)
A&M Records
1416 N. LaBrea Ave.
Hollywood, CA 90028
Format: Cassette, LP, CD
Target Ages: 5–8
Material: Imaginative songs about family life and the world we live in; all by Tom
Chapin and John Forster except where noted
Vocals: Tom Chapin; children's chorus and Judy Collins on "Rounds," "This Pretty
Planet," and "Together Tomorrow"
Vocal Style: Rich folk-style
Instrumentation: Guitar, banjo, keyboard, fiddle, concertina, drums, harmonica,
woodwinds, brass, piano, strings

We couldn't stock enough copies of *Family Tree* at the East Woods School Book
Fair. An outstanding collection of mostly original songs that reflect reverence for
humanity and ecology, it is an eloquent vehicle for Tom's warm folk-based skills
and the personal charisma that has made him such a valued television host. With
lyrical, humorous, magnetic songs that reflect family life from both children's and
parents' point of view, as well as human-sized songs about global issues, this is a
recording to be savored by the entire family.

Highlights include "Parade Came Marching," which offers humorous sound
effects for children to sing as they imagine marching through the rain; "Nick of
Time," which describes how kids wait until the last second to show up when
there's something their parents want them to do; "Rounds," exuberantly sung with
help from Judy Collins and a chorus of children; "Long Way Home," a lighthearted
fantasy about why a child is late arriving home; "Big Rock Candy Mountain," the
traditional hobo song, which Tom has updated for kids with delicious imagery
and lyrics; "Someone's Gonna Use It," a rock 'n' roll explanation of why we should
take care of the water, land, and air; "Family Tree," a joyous celebration of cultural
diversity (using his own family to illustrate how cultures blend through generations,
Tom has created an instant classic that families and schoolchildren will love to
sing); the eloquent and melodious "Pretty Planet," where, joined by Judy Collins
and a chorus of schoolchildren, Tom has created a memorable ode to Earth; and
"Don't Make Me," which reflects a child's desperation at being overwhelmed by
the demands of school. (While Tom's delivery is tongue-in-cheek, this last song

describes a very real and painful issue for some early-elementary listeners which sensitive parents and educators should treat with respect and attention.)

Also by Tom Chapin on A&M Records: *Moonboat.*

Rick Charette

Singer, songwriter, educator Rick Charette creates songs with catchy tunes and humorous, literate lyrics that address the needs and issues of early-elementary-age children. Rick's gentle, unpretentious voice is enhanced by spirited, electric accompaniment, making his recordings delightful for intergenerational listening.

Where Do My Sneakers Go at Night? (1987)
Pine Point Records
P.O. Box 901
Windham, ME 04062
Format: Cassette, LP
Age Appeal: 5–9
Material: Songs about daily experiences and fantasies written from a child's point of view; a lyrics and activity sheet included
Vocals: Rick Charette and children's chorus
Vocal Style: Gentle folk-rock
Instrumentation: Guitars, keyboards, percussion, saxophone

With the sounds of sneakers racing off to the playground by themselves, "Where Do My Sneakers Go at Night?" has to be one of the funniest family-listening songs ever written. Additional highlights include "I Hate My Name," in which Rick imagines himself living in Mexico, France, Africa, and China; "Missing Sock," an on-target song that describes the eternal search and some possible solutions to the mystery that we have all pondered; "Broken Donuts," which helps ease the frustration of always being left with fragments; and "When I'm with My Dad," in which Rick describes the good times he has with his own father.

I've Got Super Power (1986)
Educational Activities, Inc.
P.O. Box 392
Freeport, NY 11520
Format: Cassette, LP

Age Appeal: 3½–8
Material: Upbeat yet frank songs promoting personal safety through assertiveness, independent thinking, and decision-making skills; includes a lyrics sheet and suggestions for follow-up activities and discussions
Vocals: Rick Charette and children's chorus
Vocal Style: Folk/pop
Instrumentation: Guitars, drums, keyboard, saxophone, synthesizer

Sensitive and straightforward, this recording gives specific messages to kids about how to reduce their vulnerability to abuse. With its singable, contemporary-sounding songs and catchy pop music, it emphasizes the importance of independent thinking and inspires kids to appreciate their own instincts and rights. A literate, humanistic recording, *I've Got Super Power* is a wonderful musical tool for attentive, concerned adults to use when helping preschool and elementary-age children to cope effectively with the world they live in.

Highlights include "I've Got Super Power," "No! I Won't Get into Your Car," "We Never Keep a Secret for All of Our Lives," "Good Touch–Bad Touch," and "It's Going to Be Hard to Tell My Parents." After listening to this recording together, adults should be prepared to have honest, in-depth discussions with their children.

In addition to the recordings described above, Rick Charette has produced *Alligators in the Elevator* and *Bubble Gum,* available from Educational Activities.

The Children of Selma

Who Will Speak for the Children? (1987)
Rounder Records
1 Camp St.
Cambridge, MA 02140
Format: Cassette, LP, CD
Age Appeal: All ages
Target Ages: 5–14
Material: Eloquent, moving, uplifting songs by Rose Sanders; lyric sheet included
Vocals: Twenty-four children from Selma, ages two to twenty; solos by Ife Majors, Malika Sanders, Eddie Blue, Marcus Fuller, Frank Carter, James Anderson, Sarah Jones

Vocal Style: Elegant, soaring ensemble singing
Instrumentation: Piano, drums, percussion

Broadcasting messages of struggle and hope, *Who Will Speak for the Children?* is filled with powerful songs describing experiences of being young, poor, and black in a world of frustratingly unequal opportunity. The music is rich and full, with no apologies for youth.

Written by Rose Saunders, produced by Cathy Fink and Jane Sapp, directed by Jane Sapp, and performed by twenty-four children from Selma, Alabama, "the historic city where memories of the civil rights movement continue as living history,"* *Who Will Speak for the Children?* deserves classic status. Going far beyond the black experience, it eloquently addresses the struggle for human freedom and decency that continues to enslave all people.

Jesse Jackson has said that this recording offers "harmonic messages of peace, justice, and love that could transform the world if the world would listen." As I see it, if *every* teacher and parent and *every* elementary and middle-school child in the country listened to and sang along with this recording regularly, the music and messages could effect some real live improvements in human conditions around the world.

Titles on this moving recording include "Unite, Children," "We Grow Up Young," "Black Is Beautiful," "I Just Want to Be Me," "Someone Died for Me," "Vote for Me," "Who Will Speak for the Children," "Hello, Friends," "Shoo, Child," "Try Looking Up," "I Think of You," and "If Children Ruled the World."

Jon Crosse

Lullabies Go Jazz (1985)
Jazz Cat Productions
345 S. McDowell Blvd., Suite 203
Petaluma, CA 94952
Format: Cassette, LP, CD
Age Appeal: All ages
Target Ages: Newborn to toddler
Material: Top-notch, gentle jazz interpretations of classic lullabies

---

* From the record jacket.

Musicians: Jon Crosse, Clare Fischer, Putter Smith, Luis Conte
Instrumentation: soprano, alto and tenor saxophones, piano, bass, percussion

Subtitled "Sweet Sounds for Sweet Dreams," this innovative recording was conceived by saxophonist Jon Crosse in response to his infant daughter's determination to stay awake around the clock. In addition to being applauded by childhood specialists, *Lullabies Go Jazz* is being hailed by jazz musicians and critics for its superb musicianship. The *CMJ New Music Report* has said of it: "The future of jazz depends more on the education of our young than on the re-education of our adults, and this wholesome, untainted production should serve both ends and enjoy a long, healthy life." "This is music that a jazz fan can really relax to," said Ira Sabin, publisher of *Jazz Times*. "It's a classy album."

Tunes include "Brahms's Lullaby," "All the Pretty Little Horses," "Sleep, Baby, Sleep," "When You Wish Upon a Star," "Rock-a-Bye Baby," "Hush, Little Baby," "Twinkle, Twinkle, Little Star," and "All Night, All Day."

Charlotte Diamond

Charlotte Diamond sings songs that range from traditional to contemporary, from the serious to the humorous, in a variety of energetic musical styles. Her crystalline soprano voice exudes warmth, enthusiasm, and an understanding of contemporary sounds and issues.

Diamond's love of language and concern for world and family peace and understanding have come together in a major way. Her first album, *10 Carrot Diamond,* earned her a Juno award, Canada's version of the Grammy, making her an instant best-selling children's performer in British Columbia. Her second album, *Diamond in the Rough,* was a Juno nominee. She has also recorded *Qu'il y ait toujours le soleil* in French and *Diamonds and Dragons.*

By singing in French, Spanish, and a smattering of other languages (including Russian and Chinese), Diamond adds an extra dimension to her recordings. "If you teach a child another language while they're young, they're apt to be more tolerant," she explains.

And Charlotte Diamond makes it fun and easy to get involved. By translating songs such as "I Am a Pizza" into French and rewriting the Spanish-language "La

Bamba," she presents material that is irresistible. Her skillful yet lighthearted delivery makes it feel natural to sing along.

While children will not become proficient in French or Spanish from singing a few lines of a song, they will be better prepared and more eager to re-create the same sounds in the classroom if they have enjoyed them through the rhythm and melody of music.

The words are printed on the album and cassette packages so that parents and teachers can use them to expand language exposure.

10 Carrot Diamond (1985)

Hug Bug Music Inc.
6251 Chatsworth Rd.
Richmond, B.C., Canada V7C 3S4
Format: Cassette, LP
Age Appeal: 4–9
Material: Traditional and contemporary child-oriented songs, sung primarily in English but also in French, Spanish, and a smattering of German, Russian, and Cantonese
Vocals: Charlotte Diamond and children's chorus
Vocal Style: Warm, zesty, clear folk-pop soprano
Instrumentation: Guitar with additional backups

"Four Hugs a Day" is a cornerstone of Charlotte Diamond's philosophy of family togetherness. Sung here in English and later on the recording in French, it's upbeat and highly contagious, so be prepared to do plenty of singing and to give and get plenty of hugs.

Additional highlights include "I Wanna Be a Dog," the hilarious Barry Louis Polisar classic; "La Bamba," the rousing traditional song, to which Charlotte Diamond has added new lyrics so you and your children can enjoy singing a great song that finally makes sense; "Octopus," which describes the underwater food chain as the octopus eats the slippery fish, the tuna eats the octopus, the great white shark eats the tuna, and the humongous whale eats the shark, burps, and politely excuses himself; "I Am a Pizza," the kids' classic by Peter Alsop describing the process of making a pizza, with a call-and-response structure that makes it a perfect vehicle for introducing a new language; and "May There Always Be Sunshine," a touching contemporary creation based on the words of a Russian school child sung by Diamond with verses in French, Spanish, German, and Cantonese.

Jonathan Edwards

Little Hands (1987)

American Melody Records
P.O. Box 270
Guilford, CT 06347
Format: Cassette
Age Appeal: 3–8
Material: Traditional, updated, and original songs
Vocalist: Jonathan Edwards
Vocal Style: Folk-rock
Instrumentation: Guitar, banjo, harmonica, mandolin, and fiddle

If gentle folk-rock is your thing (as it is mine), this album is heaven sent. You may recognize the name Jonathan Edwards from the seventies, when he had his fifteen minutes of glory with a hit song called "Sunshine." Pop fame, as it is wont to do, waned quickly; but this man's talent has not. On *Little Hands* Jonathan Edwards sounds great. Backing up Edwards's expressive tenor voice is a wonderful bluegrass band. Elegantly produced by Phil Rosenthal, this is a recording I listen to even when there are no children around.

The first song, "Winken, Blinken and Nod," is one of the all-time best in the world of children's classics. It's based on a poem by Eugene Field, and if you have missed hearing it so far, Edwards's version is a magnetic introduction. Other traditional songs (occasionally updated) include "Stewball," "Children, Go Where I Send Thee," "Old Jim," and the delightfully revolting "Flies in the Buttermilk." The rest of the album contains contemporary compositions, including the spirited "Red Light / Green Light" and Edwards's own "My Little Girl," a touching song about a father's love for his daughter and how she helps him deal with separation.

Terrence Farrell

In this unusual collection, virtuoso classical guitarist Terrence Farrell has skillfully created a gossamer sound, sensitively interweaving classical compositions and traditional lullabies with a light, contemporary flavor. While the listening is easy, it is also elegant.

Lullaby Classics (1985)
Troubadour Records
P.O. Box 6543
Carmel, CA 93921
Format: Cassette
Age Appeal: All ages
Target age: Newborn–4
Material: Traditional lullabies as well as compositions by classical masters
Vocals: None
Style: Rich and relaxing instrumental music
Instrumentation: Terrence Farrell on guitar, Stephen Tosh on keyboards, Jacqueline Rosen on flute, and Patty Pettit on mandolin

Selections include Brahms's "Lullaby," Schumann's "Doll's Cradle Song," Grieg's "By the Cradle," Satie's Gymnopédie #1, Pachelbel's Canon in D, "Greensleeves," "Hush, Little Baby," Debussy's "Clair de lune," and Fauré's Pavane.

John M. Feierabend

Early-childhood-music specialist and Kodály expert John M. Feierabend believes in the importance of early and rich musical dialogue between infants and their parents. Because he sees this all-important tradition being undermined by the simultaneous loss of the extended family and the rise of our hurry-up, high-tech society, he has compiled *Music for Very Little People*.

To inspire parents' musical communication with their infants and toddlers, Feierabend has assembled a collection of simple songs and chants that will remind parents of songs they heard themselves as babies or introduce them to others that they may not have heard. The structured recording, pleasantly narrated and sung by Luan Saunders, gives specific and valuable suggestions to parents on how to enrich communication with their infants.

Music for Very Little People: 50 Playful Activities for Infants and Toddlers (1986)

Boosey and Hawkes, Inc.
200 Smith Street
Farmingdale, NY 11735
Format: Cassette
Age Appeal: 6 months–18 months
Material: Traditional activity rhymes, songs, and lullabies for an adult and baby to share; 75-page songbook and activity guide included, with drawings by Gary M. Kramer
Vocals: Luan Saunders
Vocal Style: Tuneful, direct, appropriately homey
Instrumentation: A capella and simple guitar accompaniments

Music for Very Little People is a large collection of short rhymes and songs, organized by headings—"Bounces," "Wiggles," "Tickles," "Tapping," "Clapping," "Circles," "Lullabies." Each section begins with suggested movements for parents to use as they listen to the recording with their babies. Parents may want to use this recording a few sections at a time, choosing different activities for different times of the day or as their children mature. "Bounces," "Wiggles," and "Tickles" on side 1 and "Lullabies" on side 2 are appropriate for young babies (provided they respond positively), while "Clapping" and "Circles" on side 2 are appropriate for toddlers.

Highlights among the more than fifty short offerings on *Music for Very Little People* include "Trot to Boston," "Ride a Cock Horse," "Dance to Your Daddy," "Round and Round the Haystack," "Slowly, Slowly," "The Bumble Bee," "Whoops Johnny!," "Clap Clap Clap Your Hands," "Peas Porridge Hot," "Allee Galloo," "The Pretty Moon," and "Baby's Boat."

Cathy Fink

While Cathy Fink has the distinction of being the first woman to win the West Virginia Old Time Banjo Contest in the thirty-two years of its existence, her talents go way beyond great banjo picking. An accomplished fiddler, guitar player, and yodeler, she is also a charismatic song stylist and a thoughtful, determined educator.

Cathy's recordings for children have received awards from Parents' Choice and the American Library Association as well as rave reviews from publications such as *The Washington Post*. In 1984 *Ms.* magazine placed *Grandma Slid Down the Mountain* on its list of "Top Ten Toys of the Year," all chosen because they were "nonsexist, nonracist, nonageist . . . challenge intelligence and imagination, and [are] just plain fun."

Cathy Fink is an active concert performer, so once you and your children fall in love with her albums, you may want to contact her office to see if she has planned a tour through your area. If you help schedule family concerts for your school, library, or community, Cathy Fink is a person to catch.

Grandma Slid Down the Mountain (1984)

Rounder Records
1 Camp St.
Cambridge, MA 02140
Format: Cassette, LP, CD
Age Appeal: 3 and up
Material: Traditional and contemporary songs, humorous, offbeat, and contemporary in their point of view
Vocals: Cathy Fink, with Marcy Marxer
Vocal style: Down-to-earth American folk singing, energetic yodeling, and lovely forties-style harmonies
Instrumentation: virtuoso banjo, guitar, and fiddle

Yodeling is one of those magical combinations of sounds that fascinate children and other playful people. On *Grandma Slid Down the Mountain* Cathy Fink shares her expertise in a way that will have you and your children yodeling along with the title song.

The fun and stimulation continue as the album moves through a lively collection of familiar folk tunes, including "New River Train" and "Oh! Susannah." Also included are lesser-known contemporary compositions such as "What Does Your Mother Do?," a celebration of working mothers written by Si Kahn; the fabulous "Peanut Butter and Jelly" chant, which so neatly defines the process of making a sandwich; and "Brush Your Teeth," which may encourage your child to spend more time with the toothbrush; as well as "I'd Like to Be a Cowgirl," "A Flea in a Fly in a Flu," "The Jazzy Three Bears," and "Cuckoo Rock."

When the Rain Comes Down (1987)

Rounder Records
Format: Cassette, LP, CD
Age Appeal: 4 and up
Material: Original and traditional songs highlighting important themes, including understanding equality, sharing, and acknowledging basic processes such as making friends, banjo playing, and baking
Vocals: Cathy Fink, with Marcy Marxer, Mary Chapin Carpenter, and children's chorus
Vocal style: Down-to-earth folk, with delicate harmonies
Instrumentation: Acoustic guitar, banjo, electric guitar, piano, saxophone, mouth bow, synthesizer, drums, including steel drums, congas, drum machine, and emulator

Cathy Fink's newest album on Rounder Records is an exciting collection of songs and styles. In addition to delivering songs in her forthright folk voice, Cathy, with the help of her friends Marcy Marxer and Mary Chapin Carpenter, dishes up satiny-smooth fifties country-western sounds and energetic harmonies inspired by the Andrews Sisters. Except for the ode to cookies, done in a trendy rap style that places the album firmly in the present, you might think that this recording is a thirty-year-old classic rather than a gem of the eighties.

Beginning with the title song and running right through the recording, the selections are both entertaining and thought provoking. This is an album that never lets up. "When the Rain Comes Down," destined to become a classic, is an elegant tribute to human equality. The irresistible gossamer accompaniment on the hammered dulcimer will compel you to sing along. You'll miss it so much when it's over that you might even replay it immediately.

"Magic Penny," a 1955 Malvina Reynolds classic, is given a glorious incarnation by Cathy Fink as she backs it up with steel drum, children's chorus, and scat-style vocals. If you haven't yet heard "Magic Penny," this is a great introduction. If it's already in the family repertoire, you will enjoy Cathy's delightful interpretation.

Cathy delivers the humorous "Susie and the Alligator" in a wry tone. A cautionary tale with a bizarre Maurice Sendak–esque twist, it imparts an important message for people of all ages: describe life as you see it, no matter how hard it is to be heard, no matter how others resist the truth.

"Alphabet Boogie" swings with forties-style energy and harmonies, complete with piano, sax, and electric guitar accompaniment. Can you meet Cathy's challenge and sing the alphabet backwards?

"Rock, Rock, Old Joe Clark" is a great showcase for Cathy's skill on the banjo. If you love the sounds of the banjo (as I do), you'll adore this cut. If you're not yet energized by banjo music, perhaps it's because you have yet to hear Cathy Fink play.

The mellow electric-guitar accompaniment on "Uncle Noah's Ark" creates such a lively barnyard feeling that it's easy to imagine Uncle Noah in his red plaid shirt and old straw hat surrounded by his menagerie.

"Martin Luther King" is yet another cut on this album well on its way to classic status. With strong piano accompaniment and gospel-style vocal backups, Cathy's call-and-response tribute to Martin Luther King will get everyone singing and thinking and doing.

Cathy's musical and vocal treatment of "Cookies" brings her firmly into the eighties and helps identify rap as an important storytelling style much in the same tradition as the talking blues. With a full regalia of synthesized sounds and a Cookie Monster sound-alike doing vocal backups, Cathy articulates the process of cookie making and eating.

"Betty Botter" is a humorous, tongue-twisting story that everyone will want to try. Meeting the tongue-twister challenge is a great example of education through play. In order to succeed, the listener must recognize and imitate the pattern and rhythms of language and speech.

"Skip to My Lou" is such a childhood workhorse that you may be surprised, as I was, to see it listed on such an innovative recording. Let me assure you that the haunting mouth-bow instrumentation and Cathy's subtle delivery transform it into an elegant new song.

Cathy's love of her instrument is evident in "The Banjo Song" as she describes songs, people, and the process of strumming.

Backed up with a smooth, upbeat acoustic guitar, snare drum, and delicate vocal harmonies, Cathy on "Shakin' Hands" reaffirms the importance of this form of communication.

"Whoever Shall Have Some Good Peanuts" is a traditional song with a rousing new treatment by Cathy that will inspire the kids on the block to share their favorite foods.

"Seven Days to Rock" is "Rock Around the Clock" reinterpreted for the days of the week, with an electric-guitar backup and perfect vocal harmonies that will transport you back to 1955.

After all this high energy, the quiet banjo, hammered dulcimer, and mellow woodblocks establish a restful tone for the final two songs. "As Soon As We All Cook Sweet Potatoes" is a gentle song about the end of one day and the beginning of the next.

The soothing "Happy Trails," made famous by Roy Rogers and Dale Evans, is sure to find a new generation of fans through the romantic cowgirl rendition performed by Cathy Fink and her friends Marcy Marxer and Mary Chapin Carpenter.

Gemini

"If the Pied Piper had been twins, odds are he would have been Gemini," said *The Detroit News* of this exuberant musical duo. Blending crisp, harmonic singing and toe-tapping instrumentals, Gemini's energizing sound, reminiscent of the Lime-liters, is supercharged by tradition.

Twin brothers Sandor and Laszlo Slomovits, born in Hungary, immigrated to the United States in 1959 at age ten after living in Israel for three years. Their father, a cantor, began early to teach them a wide variety of music.

While both of them have degrees from the University of Rochester (San in history and Las in English), the Slomovits brothers discovered during their college years that they were happiest when they made music together. With their glorious, matched voices, accompanying themselves on an impressive range of instruments (including the guitar, the pennywhistle, the fiddle, and the mandolin), they formed Gemini and began performing for adult audiences.

In the late 1970s, when Gemini was invited by principals and teachers to perform in schools, the brothers realized that young audiences were extremely enthusiastic about their music. Since then, they have released three critically acclaimed albums for family listening on which they combine traditional and contemporary music from around the world with their own compositions. In addition, they have arranged and recorded eleven albums of international ethnic folk-dance music for the High/Scope Educational Research Foundation which are being used in schools throughout the country to teach movement and dance to young children.

Good Mischief (1982)

Gemini Records
2000 Penncraft Ct.
Ann Arbor, MI 48103
Format: Cassette, LP
Age Appeal: All ages
Target Ages: 4–9
Material: Traditional and original songs sung in a variety of languages, recorded live in concert
Vocals: Sandor and Laszlo Slomovits
Vocal Style: Crisp folk harmonies sung with lively accompaniment
Instrumentation: Guitar, violin, bones, bodhran (Irish drum), clay drums, fiddle-sticks, pennywhistle, bowed psaltery, banjo, jaw harp, harmonica

Highlights of side 1, which has an energetic vocal sound, include "The Marvelous Toy," "I'm Gonna Tell," "A Place in the Choir," and "Zum Gali Gali." Side 2 is primarily spirited instrumental music.

Pulling Together (1986)

Gemini Records
Format: Cassette, LP
Age Appeal: All ages
Target Ages: 4–9
Material: Traditional and original songs sung in a variety of languages
Vocals: Sandor and Laszlo Slomovits and children's chorus
Vocal Style: Clear, exuberant folk harmonies with lively accompaniment
Instrumentation: Guitar, fiddle, mandolin, pennywhistle, flute, banjo, Autoharp, tambourine, bones

Highlights of the award-winning *Pulling Together* include "Michael Row the Boat Ashore," "May There Always Be Sunshine," "You Can't Make a Turtle Come Out," "Yellow Submarine," and "This Land Is Your Land."

Tom Glazer

One of America's greatest balladeers, Tom Glazer began his career in the 1940s singing with other soon-to-be legendary figures, including Woody Guthrie, Josh White, Leadbelly, and Burl Ives. While there are several more visible personalities on the children's music scene these days, to my mind there is no greater superstar than Tom Glazer, the man who thirty-five years ago pioneered music for family listening that we cherish today.

In the late 1940s Tom Glazer discovered that in addition to his rich, clear, singing voice he possessed a reverence for the music of childhood and a unique talent that enabled him to draw young listeners into the spirit and energy of music. Collecting traditional folk songs from around the world as well as writing original compositions, Tom Glazer began to perform and record music for very young audiences.

Today, with more than twenty-five recordings to his credit, including *Music for Ones and Twos, Let's Sing Fingerplays,* and *Children's Greatest Hits,* Tom Glazer's energetic, folk-oriented sound and the interactive, sing-along, play-along approach can be identified as a major building block of today's "new" music for children. In the introduction to his book *Tom Glazer's Treasury of Folk Songs for the Family,* he explained: "The first time I sang before an audience of children, I noticed immediately an inability on their part to refrain from participating. This was at first somewhat disconcerting, and being unable to stifle their effervescence, I gave in to it in self-defense. I discovered that if to sing for children is purgatory, to sing for AND WITH THEM is a kind of paradise, complete with noise, colds, character defects and unpredictable attention spans."

For parents of infants and toddlers, I recommend listening to at least one of Tom Glazer's recordings for youngest listeners. Tom's ability to present clear, appropriately paced musical sounds and images is remarkable. While an adult would not choose to listen to these seemingly spare recordings alone, the parent of a child who is beginning to assemble the phrases and words of speech will appreciate the simple yet inspired material offered by Tom as it supplies invaluable opportunities for fun and growth.

For parents and their toddler, preschool-, and kindergarten-age children, I suggest listening to at least one of Tom Glazer's activity, game, or greatest hits recordings. Tom offers important traditional American songs with energy and humor, and his tempo and vocal range are perfectly suited to youngest listeners.

Music for Ones and Twos (1972)
CMS Records
226 Washington St.
Mount Vernon, NY 10553
Format: Cassette, LP
Age Appeal: 18 months–3 years
Material: Simple songs, rhymes, and games for youngest listeners
Vocals: Tom Glazer
Vocal Style: Clear, expressive, and elegant
Instrumentation: Guitar

Highlights from this classic recording include "Nice," "Bye Bye," "Where Are Your Eyes?," "What Does Baby See?," "What Does Baby Hear?," "Clap Hands," and "Baby's Bath."

Activity and Game Songs, Volumes 1 and 2 (1973)
CMS Records
Format: Cassette, LP
Age Appeal: 2½–4
Material: Traditional songs for singing and playing along
Vocals: Tom Glazer and "600 Howling, Screaming, Insane, Delirious Children"
Vocal Style: Expressive, melodious folk
Instrumentation: Guitar

Volume 1 of this exuberant collection includes "Jimmie Crack Corn," "Jennie Jenkins," "Skip to My Lou," "The Fox," "Put Your Finger in the Air," and "Pick a Bale."

Volume 2 contains Tom Glazer's classic creation "On Top of Spaghetti" as well as "Come Down the Aisle," "The Bus Song," "The New Rock Candy Mountain," "The Name Song," "I Know an Old Lady," and "I Ride an Old Paint."

Let's Sing Fingerplays (1977)
CMS Records
Format: Cassette, LP
Age Appeal: 2–4
Material: Activity songs with clear narrative instructions for young children
Vocals: Tom Glazer

Vocal Style: Clear, rich, enthusiastic
Instrumentation: Guitar and rhythm instruments

Highlights from this interactive recording include "Grandma's Spectacles," "The Bear Went Over the Mountain," "Bingo," "The Bus Song," "Come On and Join Into the Game," "Eentsy Weentsy Spider," and "Eye Winker, Tom Tinker, Chin Chopper."

Children's Greatest Hits, Volume 1 (1977)
CMS Records
Format: Cassette, LP
Age Appeal: 3–5
Material: Traditional songs for children
Vocals: Tom Glazer
Vocal Style: Rich, clear, and energetic
Instrumentation: Guitar

Selections include "This Old Man," "Rudolph the Red-Nosed Reindeer," "The Little White Duck," "Down at the Station," and "He's Got the Whole World in His Hands."

Red Grammer

When he's not touring the world as lead singer for the famed folk group the Limeliters, Red Grammer keeps busy writing and performing for family audiences. A warm and lively performer, he can be seen in concert as part of the Disney Channel "Kaleidoscope" series.

Teaching Peace (1986)
The Children's Group
The Children's Book Store Distribution
561 Bloor St. West, Suite 300
Toronto, Ontario, Canada M5S 1Y6
Format: Cassette
Target Ages: 3–6
Material: Original songs that celebrate diversity, equality, humanity, and imagination
Vocals: Red Grammer with backup vocals by adults and children
Vocal Style: Soaring vocals reminiscent of John Denver

Instrumentation: Guitars, mandolin, harmonica, cello, keyboards, drums, bass, piccolo

Making a pretty strong claim with its title, *Teaching Peace* turns out to be a collection of songs promoting the premise that global peace begins at home. Sung with sparkle and sincerity by Red Grammer, the contemporary, high-energy songs offer tools for enhancing communication between individuals. The soaring music invites repeated listening; and if we absorb even a quarter of what Red Grammer has to tell us, our own homes, at the very least, will be much more peaceful and satisfying places in which to live.

Song highlights include "Teaching Peace," "Places in the World," "Use a Word," "Shake Your Brains," and "With Two Wings."

Also by Red Grammer are *Can You Sound Just Like Me?* and *Grammer in the Schools*.

Howard Hanger

Howard Hanger, a jazz musician and ordained Methodist minister, shares his deep love of jazz through his recordings *For Kids Only* and *For Kids Only 2*. Interspersing twangy narratives throughout both recordings, Hanger stresses to young listeners his feelings about jazz: jazz is rhythm, jazz is being free, jazz is having fun. "Jazz has always been the domain of adults and smoke-filled clubs and concert halls," Hanger has said. "But jazz at its best is kids at their best—free, loose, and having a good time. Jazz is a vehicle for letting them express themselves. Jazz should start in the crib."

Hanger, who also has recorded a Christmas album and recordings for adult audiences, spends several months a year traveling throughout the country with his Jazz Fantasy, giving performances in classrooms and school auditoriums.

For Kids Only (1984) and **For Kids Only 2** (1986)
Howard Hanger Jazz Fantasy
31 Park Ave.
Asheville, NC 28801
Format: Cassette, LP
Age Appeal: 4–8
Material: Traditional and contemporary songs interpreted with fresh jazz sounds

Vocals: Howard Hanger and friends
Vocal Style: Friendly, gravelly-voiced, with clearly articulated lyrics
Instrumentation: Piano, trumpet, flugelhorn, bass, violin, synthesizer, drums, assorted percussion

On *For Kids Only* Howard Hanger's religious leanings are apparent on "Noah Found Grace" and "Forbidden Fruit," but in general he has chosen traditional and contemporary secular songs which he uses to enhance his descriptions of rhythm in jazz. Additional highlights include his jazz interpretations of "Apples and Bananas," "Mr. Bojangles," and "Jazz and Rhythm."

For Kids Only 2 is an award-winning collection of traditional and contemporary songs celebrating the jazz tradition. Enhanced by lively narration, this fresh-sounding secular recording can provide delightful listening for children and adults together. Songs of special note are "Syncopation Swing," a sing-along that helps listeners understand syncopated sound; "It's Fun to Be Human," an upbeat, positive song about individuality; "Field Holler Blues," a narrative describing how slaves gave birth to jazz; "Sing Like Louis," depicting the life and musical style of Louis Armstrong; and "I'm a Little Cookie," the Larry Penn classic about appreciating human imperfections, sung with an innovative and effective jazz treatment.

Bill Harley

With his remarkable memory and great gift for communication, Bill Harley contributes a new dimension of understanding and enjoyment to the lives of the children and adults who are lucky enough to hear his songs and stories. Whether sharing his traditional and original tales or recounting his childhood experiences so that them seem like they just happened, Bill has the uncanny ability to reaffirm life for his listeners, be they five or fifty. Humor, empathy, intelligence, and reality all radiate from Bill, both on his recordings and during the more than two hundred live performances he gives each year. If Bill is performing near you, be sure your family is part of the audience. For a concert schedule or to arrange a Bill Harley performance in your area, contact Debbie Block, Round River Productions.

When selecting Bill Harley recordings, be careful to consult the age-appeal ratings.

Monsters in the Bathroom (1985)
Round River Records
301 Jacob St.
Seekonk, MA 02771
Format: Cassette, LP
Age Appeal: 4–10
Material: Traditional and contemporary songs and stories that stress the value of individuality and freedom
Vocals: Bill Harley with vocal backup
Vocal style: Engaging, clear, melodious, folk inspired
Instrumentation: Guitar, piano, saxophones, spoons, flutes, accordion

While influenced by the legendary Pete Seeger, Bill Harley has developed an important charismatic style all his own. On *Monsters in the Bathroom* Bill has assembled a collection of traditional and original songs and stories that transmit a variety of important themes. Highlights include the humorous round "Black Socks"; "What's the Matter With You?," a well-targeted song about how to stand up for your right to be yourself; "When I Grow Up," sung with audience participation, which sends the message to kids that their lives are filled with possibilities and choices; "The Billboard Song," in which Bill mismatches familiar and advertising slogans.

The title track, "Monsters in the Bathroom," contains silly sounds and images that children love as well as a humorous, fun-to-sing chorus. Singing from a child's point of view, Bill builds fear and tension as he imagines the worst from noises he hears in the dark. Mom, remembering her own childhood fears, steps in to save the day.

Brought from Thailand by storyteller David Holt, "The Freedom Bird" is a fascinating parable of power, destruction, and the durable spirit of freedom. Bill enhances the effect of this graphic story of a hunter who shoots and slaughters a bird who will not die by inviting young listeners to taunt at the appropriate times, "Na na nana nana na."

"Abiyoyo" is based on Pete Seeger's creation of the same name, developed from a South African lullaby. It is the story of an incorrigible boy and his unpopular magician father who, banished to the edge of town for their misdeeds, become heroes when they save the town from destruction by the monster Abiyoyo. Bill Harley ably passes this satisfying tale on to another generation.

50 Ways to Fool Your Mother (1986)

Round River Records
Format: Cassette, LP
Age Appeal: 5–10
Material: Contemporary and traditional songs
Vocals: Bill Harley with children's chorus
Vocal Style: Engaging, clear, melodious, folk based
Instrumentation: Acoustic guitar and electric guitars, banjo, body sounds (juba), piano, keyboard, drums, saxophone

On *50 Ways to Fool Your Mother* Bill Harley combines traditional tunes of freedom and brotherhood with his own compositions. While he blends humor and reality into his own tunes, he also infuses the traditional ones with a fresh, contemporary flavor, making a much-needed pitch to reach children who, captivated by the outstanding title song, would not otherwise listen to "uncool" folk-oriented music, however important.

Other strong original selections are "There Goes My Brother Again," which describes the frustrations of having a younger brother; "My Dog Sam," which recounts loving memories of a favorite pet and deals with facing the sadness of loss; and "Havin' a Party," a rock 'n' roll number that expresses outrage at being excluded from a parents' party. Other numbers delivered with gusto include the traditional "I'm on My Way," Ruth Pelham's "Under One Sky," and Oscar Brand's "When I First Came to This Land."

Dinosaurs Never Say Please (1987)

Round River Records
Format: Cassette, LP
Age Appeal: 5–8
Material: Original and traditional stories
Vocals: Bill Harley
Vocal Style: Charismatic narrative
Instrumentation: Guitar

Injected with Bill Harley's intimate, light tone, these tales can be appreciated for their humorous story lines or used to address timely issues.

"Dinosaurs Never Say Please," which fills side 1, is a lushly detailed narrative about Jimmy, a little boy who is angered by the indignities he must endure.

Overbearing siblings, cruel rules in the school lunch room, and a mother who demands good manners are all grounds for his unquenchable anger. When Jimmy wishes to the tooth fairy to become an all-powerful Tyrannosaurus rex, his wish is granted. But a life of power through intimidation is fun for just so long, and being a dinosaur has physical drawbacks as well. Glad to turn back into a boy, Jimmy faces life with a mellower attitude.

Highlights of side 2 include "I'm Busy," the antithesis to the traditional tale of the boy who cried wolf. Through musical dialogue, a child repeatedly warns his father about the monster that is destroying the house. Dad, always too distracted to pay attention, is finally swallowed down by the monster with a juicy gulp. The story ends with an unspoken but well-deserved "I told you so."

Also of special note is "Bojabi," a traditional African folktale told by Bill with his own original music. A young turtle has alienated himself from the animal community by endlessly singing a little tune which he has written but never finished. When drought threatens the animal population and no one can manage to remember the important message from the lion that can save their lives, the little turtle finally finishes his song and saves the world. In the telling of "Bojabi," Bill continues to develop his important philosophy: help comes from the most unexpected sources, and music has many powers. Two other striking examples of this theme in Bill's work can be heard in "Zanzibar" (on *Cool in School*) and "Abiyoyo" (on *Monsters in the Bathroom*).

Cool in School: Tales from Sixth Grade (1987)

Round River Records
Format: Cassette, LP
Age Appeal: 10–15
Material: Hilarious, original tales, punctuated with charismatic singing, which talk about what it means to be "cool," the pain of a first crush, and the eternal problem of homework procrastination
Vocals: Bill Harley
Vocal Style: Intimate narrative interwoven with catchy tunes
Instrumentation: Guitar

This innovative recording focuses on a rarely addressed period of childhood—early adolescence. Perhaps because children by the age of eleven or twelve are often so involved with Top 40 music, no one else has thought to examine this important passage of life on recordings for them. But no matter—Bill Harley has done an eye-opening job. Let's hope he has just invented a new genre.

"Cool in School," the title track, is a song that asks the eternal question "What is cool?" Backed up by doo-wop harmonies and energetic finger snapping inspired by the Coasters, Bill asks, "[Is it] the way you tie your shoes, the way you comb your hair, the superheroes hiding on your underwear?" While he offers no definitive answer, "Cool in School" acts as an introduction to the touching story about his "first crush," which follows.

"Zanzibar," which fills side 2, is a story to be shared, discussed, and enjoyed by upper-elementary- and middle-school-aged children with their parents and teachers. A twenty-five-minute story about homework excuses reminiscent of Arlo Guthrie's classic "Alice's Restaurant," it is destined to become a classic in its own right. Integrating humorous, realistic confessions of how he put off doing homework with a catchy chorus, Bill Harley makes "Zanzibar" much more than mere nostalgia.

You're in Trouble (1989)
Round River Records
Format: Cassette, LP
Target Age: 6–8
Material: Humorous and touching songs about family life
Vocals: Bill Harley, with adult backup and a chorus of third graders
Instrumentation: Guitars, piano, synthesizer, trumpet, drums, washboard, clarinet, trombone, flute, saxophone

Bill's newest, and some people's favorite. Highlights include the title song, "No School Today," "If You're Gonna Be a Grub," "Moon and Me," "Cool in School," and "Dad Threw the TV Out the Window."

Chris Holder

An active arts-in-education advocate, Chris Holder has been singing his story songs and conducting workshops for children and teachers in New York State for more than ten years. He allows his songs and stories to grow and evolve in response to his audiences, and the results have come together on two animated recordings. Chris's way of bringing people and history to life is so colorful that listeners may want to make a trip to the library to find out even more about the fascinating events he depicts.

Though his friendly style is distinctly his own, the influences of Pete Seeger and Arlo Guthrie are clear. It's reassuring to have personable, intelligent Chris Holder to carry the torch of story singing into the 1990s.

Chris Holder, Storysinger:
Tunes and Tales Both Tall and True (1982)
A Gentle Wind
P.O. Box 3103
Albany, NY 12203
Format: Cassette
Age Appeal: 5–11
Material: Traditional tales and tunes interpreted with energy and enthusiasm
Vocals: Chris Holder and children's chorus
Vocal Style: Folk
Instrumentation: Guitar and banjo

Highlights of this colorful recording include "Johnny Appleseed," an amalgam of many versions of the great American myth woven together with a delightful chorus; "The Sprightly Tailor," taken from Celtic tradition and told as a humorous, spine-tingling tale; and "Nelly Bly," one of my all-time-favorite story songs, which describes the achievements of a real-life human-rights activist and newspaper reporter who in 1889, after reading Jules Verne's fictitious account, traveled around the world in less than eighty days. This is a joyful song of self-determination that all children should have the opportunity to enjoy.

Imagination Cruise (1987)
A Gentle Wind
(See *Chris Holder, Storysinger* above for details.)

Highlighting this recording is "Wizard of the Highway," a humorous tale describing how one family learns to cope with the noise during a family car trip, based on the traditional Yiddish wisdom that people don't appreciate how good things are until they get worse. Chris has created vivid sound pictures and a singable chorus—perfect listening for a raucous family group during just such an outing.

Janet and Judy

Janet and Judy Robinson are vivacious identical twins who create recordings of original music, comedy, and characters built around educational themes. Uniquely aimed at seven-to-eleven-year-olds, their award-winning music has a high-energy, contemporary sound and rich, fact-filled lyrics.

Each fast-moving recording is structured like a radio show, with amusing banter between the sisters and their daffy cast of characters, including Miss Wixmords, who reverses syllables; Dr. Zoolittle from Australia; and Candy Gum, the valley girl who identifies the four basic food groups as soda pop, potato chips, chocolate chip cookies, and candy and gum.

The sisters, both with bachelors of science from the University of Illinois, grew up in a musical family. Although they began their professional performing careers playing in nightclubs, they now perform exclusively for young audiences in southern California. Putting on an action-packed stage show, they zip in and out of costumes to portray their characters. "We ended up in children's entertainment because it was most rewarding," says Judy, "and that's where we really seemed to shine. We really feel lucky to have this job."

Words 'N' Music (1985)

Janet and Judy Records
P.O. Box 1653
Burbank, CA 91507
Format: Cassette, LP
Age Appeal: 7–11
Material: Colorful original music enhanced by comedy and characters focused on word skills
Vocals: Janet and Judy Robinson with chorus of children
Vocal Style: Warm, infectious, eclectic style with vocals reminiscent of Diana Ross and Dolly Parton
Instrumentation: Acoustic, electric, and steel guitars, keyboards, synthesizers, fiddle, banjo, mandolin, Autoharp

Highlights of *Words 'N' Music* include "The New ABC Song," "Oh! Susannah / The Antonym Song," "The Purple People Eater," "Herb the Verb," "Saturday Night," and "Words 'n' Music."

Musical Fitness (1985)

Janet and Judy Records

(See *Words 'N' Music*, page 114, for details.)

Songs of special note on *Musical Fitness* include "Eat Good Food, Get Your Rest, and Exercise," "Go Nutrients Go," "Four Basic Foods Rap," "Keep the Sugar on the Shelf," "Fruits and Vegetables," and "Keep Movin'."

Music Almanac (1987)

Janet and Judy Records

(See *Words 'N' Music*, page 114, for details.)

Highlights include "I Like Science and Nature," "Thank a Plant," "Where Does It Come From?," "What's the Weather?," and "Nine Planets."

A Musical Tour of the Fifty States (1987)

Janet and Judy Records

(See *Words 'N' Music*, page 114, for details.)

Song selections include "Fifty States of America," "In the Hills of Tennessee," "Chicago Blues," "North Dakota, South Dakota," "M-i-s-s-i-s-s-i-p-p-i," and "Alaska, Land of the Last Frontier."

Ella Jenkins

A pioneer in the field of children's music, Ella Jenkins has been sharing her love of children and music since the 1950s. Having recorded more than twenty albums, written a theme song for the United Nations International Year of the Child, and appeared frequently on "Mister Rogers' Neighborhood" and "Sesame Street," she is one of our country's earliest and most enduring childhood-music advocates.

Beyond establishing and maintaining her career as a children's performer, over the years Ella Jenkins has given hundreds of workshops for educators on how to use music to enhance the development of children. Traveling throughout the country and the world sharing ideas and music, gathering inspiration for new songs, Ella Jenkins continues to encourage adults to expose children to music from cultures other than their own. "If we understand one another, we're less likely to fight with one another," she has said. "It may seem to children that people that they don't know and people who look different are a little odd. People can get to know each other through music, rhythms, instruments, and stories."

Ella Jenkins has a warm, compelling voice that reflects the jazz and blues influence of her childhood. Accompanying herself on the guitar, ukulele, and a collection of fascinating instruments amassed on her travels, she makes music that is elegant, inviting, and perfectly paced for young listeners.

Ella Jenkins recordings and performances always include audience participation. Whether she is singing a song about protecting animals in Africa or chanting a wonderful rhythmic childhood game, she offers direct and immediate phrases and tunes for children to sing back to her. "I could just stand up there and sing the entire time," she has said. "But it's much more fun for them to be a part, and that way they're really learning and using their imagination."

Be sure to treat yourself and your preschooler to at least one Ella Jenkins recording. For information on presenting an Ella Jenkins workshop or concert in your area, contact her manager, Bernadelle Richter, Adventures in Rhythm, 1844 North Mohawk Street, Chicago, Illinois 60614.

You'll Sing a Song and I'll Sing a Song (1966)

Smithsonian / Folkways Records
Smithsonian Institution
Office of Folklife Programs
955 L'Enfant Plaza, Suite 2600
Washington, D.C. 20560
Nationally distributed by Rounder Records
1 Camp St.
Cambridge, MA 02140
Format: Cassette, LP
Age Appeal: 5–8
Material: Original and traditional songs; lyrics included
Vocals: Ella Jenkins with members of the Urban Gateways Children's Chorus
Vocal Style: Folk
Instrumentation: Ukulele, chord lyre, finger cymbals, tone blocks

This rhythmic, interactive recording is structured for imitating as well as creating. Highlights include "You'll Sing a Song and I'll Sing a Song," "This Train," "Did You Feed My Cow?," "Miss Mary Mack," "Maori Indian Battle Chant," and "Guide Me."

I Know the Colors in the Rainbow (1981)

Educational Activities, Inc.

P.O. Box 392

Freeport, NY 11520

Format: Cassette, LP

Age Appeal: 3–5

Material: Original and traditional songs that promote cooperation and international understanding

Vocals: Ella Jenkins and "a rainbow of children from St. Vincent De Paul Center"

Instrumentation: Piano, ukulele, violin, guitar, saxophone, percussion, flute, harmonica

Reflecting her travels, especially her trip to China, *I Know the Colors in the Rainbow* is a gentle and singable collection of songs created by Ella Jenkins for preschool and home listening and singing. The rich, rhythmic, informal style will encourage children to create their own music long after they hear the recording.

Highlights include "I Know the Colors in the Rainbow," "Who Fed the Chickens?," "Bim Bom, Bim Bom," "Kaluba, Beat the Drum," "In the People's Republic of China," and "I'm Singing a Solo."

Hopping Around from Place to Place, Volume 1 (1983)

Educational Activities, Inc.

Format: Cassette, LP

Age Appeal: 4–7

Vocals: Ella Jenkins and chorus of children

Instrumentation: Piano, guitar, ukulele, accordion, bells, and percussion

Hopping Around from Place to Place contains original songs that focus on geography. Comparing the habits and traditions of people around the United States as well as in Germany, Switzerland, Hawaii, and England, Ella Jenkins creates songs that are immediately singable, fascinating, and fun.

Highlights include "I Think I'll Go to Oregon," "I'm Going to Cairo," "A German Counting Rhyme," "Climbing Up Mount Rigi," "They Play the Ukulele in Lovely Hawaii," "If You Go to London Town," and "I Know a City Called Okeechobee."

Looking Forward and Looking Back (1981)

Educational Activities, Inc.

Format: Cassette, LP

Age Appeal: 4–7
Material: Traditional and original songs and chants of childhood
Vocals: Ella Jenkins and schoolchildren
Vocal Style: Folk
Instrumentation: Ukulele, percussion, piano, and game sounds

On this ingenious recording Ella Jenkins, with the help of schoolchildren, uses the sounds of toys as rhythmic accompaniment to interactive chants and songs. Toys include jump rope, jacks, marbles, and tops. Children who hear this recording will be eager to play with the often-overlooked toys that are portrayed, so adults should be prepared to make them available.

Song highlights are "Little Sally Colors," "Little Ella Bella, Little Tommy Breen," "Lemonade Stand," "Ice Cream Soda," "Scooping Up Jacks, Shooting Marbles," "How Long Will the Top Spin?," and "Counting from One to Ten in Spanish."

Kathi and Milenko, Nancy Rumbel, and Friends

Good Morning, Good Night (1987)
Lightworks Productions
P.O. Box 676
Issaquah, WA 98027
Format: Cassette
Age Appeal: All ages
Target Ages: 3–7; side 2 also appropriate for parents, newborns, and toddlers
Material: Classic children's literature set to music plus original and traditional material; words included
Vocals: Kathi and Milenko Matanovic with help from children, including Katya Matanovic and Bethany Ward
Vocal Style: Haunting, elegant
Instrumentation (Nancy Rumbel is the primary musician): guitar, saxophone, clarinet, marimba, bells, whistles, chimes, piano, synthesizer, banjo, oboe, french horn, double ocarinas, percussion, cheng

Good Morning, Good Night, subtitled "Musical Poems and Lullabies," is a jewel of a recording. With an old-world elegance, the Matanovic family has set to music traditional poetry written by Robert Louis Stevenson, William Wordsworth, and Rudyard Kipling (to name a few of the poets), rounding out the collection with a sprinkling of traditional and original songs. With remarkable performances by adults and children alike, the result is a rich, joyous, magical recording that stands in a class by itself.

Side 1 contains upbeat activity songs that have unusual depth of sound and spirit. The children's performances, unaffected and strong, will inspire young listeners to sing along.

Side 2, designed to "summon children into the land of nod," contains gentle, haunting lullabies that parents will enjoy listening to with newborns and toddlers as well as young children.

Song highlights include "Block City" and "My Shadow," both with words by Stevenson; "The Peaceable Kingdom"; "Ladybird! Ladybird!" with words by Emily Brontë; and "When It's Dark in the Night" by Katya and Milenko Matanovic.

The Kids of Widney High

Michael Monagan, pop musician and teacher of the severely handicapped in the Los Angeles public schools, set up a songwriting class at Widney High to see if his students could write songs for the school play. A developmentally disabled group with a variety of conditions, including epilepsy, cerebral palsy, blindness, Down's syndrome, and muscular dystrophy, these children were known throughout the school as having behavior problems. Although the project took a tremendous amount of work, Michael Monagan feels that it was successful beyond his wildest dreams. As a result of his efforts, Monagan reports, "many of the behavior problems decreased and the kids have experienced a boost in self-esteem and a feeling of success and accomplishment too rare in their lives."

As an additional treat, out of this venture has come an affecting recording that can be enjoyed by people of all ages and conditions. For it Monagan created a crisp, full backup sound to enhance the determined, passionate compositions and vocals by his students.

To accompany the recording, Monagan has written a teachers' guide in which he describes the project as it developed with his students. He suggests a variety of ways musician and nonmusician educators can bring songwriting into all types of classrooms, and expresses the hope that "this basic framework can be used as a catalyst in settings that may be the same or very different from the one I've created with the kids at Widney High."

Leo Buscaglia has said, "This glowing album is a tribute to the determination of the children, the unswerving faith of Michael Monagan—their music teacher— and an educational program that does not stress limitation, only limitless possibilities."

The Kids of Widney High: Special Music from Special Kids (1989)
Rounder Records
1 Camp St.
Cambridge, MA 02140
Format: Cassette, LP
Age Appeal: All ages
Material: Hopeful, energetic original songs written and performed by developmentally disabled students; lyrics and teachers' guide included
Vocals: David Aronin, Carl Brown, Jerron Crook, Keisha Dotson, Brenda Garcia, John Insinna, Nancy Preston, Diane Reyes, Gerardo Reyes, Robert Ross, Phomma Vannaseng, Norman Williams, Tommy Yates
Instrumentation: Keyboards, guitars, drum machines, saxophone, trumpet

The concerns, hopes, and issues that affect the Kids of Widney High are universal, though rarely do children have the opportunity to articulate them with such clarity and strength. Highlights of this award-winning album include: "New Car," in which the kids describe how they would express their pride in owning a new vehicle; "Teddy Bear," a touching description of the value of this soft, furry possession; "65 Years Old," a stunning eulogy to a hardworking grandmother; "Hollywood," depicting the lure of the famous town where glamour and poverty live side by side; and "Primary Reinforcement," in which individual kids sing about their creations and skills.

Other titles include "Mirror, Mirror," "Insects," "Mayra," "Stand Up and Dance," "Throw Away the Trash," "New York," "Widney High," "Friends," and "Ride Away."

Kids on the Block

The Kids on the Block was created in 1977 by Barbara Aiello as a culmination of her eighteen years of teaching and consulting in the field of special education.

Furnishing colorful hand-and-rod puppets, teachers' guides, props, and educational tools, the Kids on the Block organization offers teachers and volunteers everything they need to create puppet shows that engage children in forthright dialogues about disabilities (cerebral palsy, mental retardation), medical conditions (epilepsy, leukemia), and social concerns (sexual abuse, substance abuse, divorce).

With the philosophy that "being different is a universal condition," the aim of the Kids on the Block is not merely to heighten understanding and awareness of the handicapped but also to help everyone accept difference in others and themselves. Barbara Aiello has said, "People haven't been made comfortable with differences. As a result, our fears cut us off from a very important segment in our society. The important thing is to realize that disabilities are not defects but rather examples of life's natural diversity that enrich us all."

To find out how you can make the Kids on the Block part of your community, write Kids on the Block, 9385-C Gerwig Lane, Columbia, Maryland 21046; or call toll free (800) 368-KIDS (continental U.S., except Maryland), or in Maryland, (301) 290-9095.

C'mon Along, We All Belong (1986)
Golden Music
Western Publishing
1220 Mound Ave.
Racine, WI 53404
Format: Cassette, LP
Age Appeal: 5 and up
Target Ages: 5–12
Material: Forthright dialogue and songs about a variety of human conditions, including cerebral palsy and blindness, produced with a full, rock sound
Vocals: The studio cast of the Kids on the Block, with a guest appearance by ROSENSHONTZ on "Go for It"
Vocal Style: Clear and powerful rock
Instrumentation: Electric guitars, keyboards, synthesizer, and percussion

On this recording, performed by the national touring cast, listeners will hear the musical story of how the students of Woodburn Elementary School are preparing a talent show to celebrate their school's reunion when a stuck-up new boy joins their group. This effective recording can be enjoyed by all children and adults on the strength of its music alone. The fact that it addresses important issues of human diversity with energy and style makes it all the more powerful a tool for expanding the horizons of every person who hears it.

Song highlights include "Kids Are Different," "Go for It," "Special People," "Blind Kid's Rap," "Charlie Brown," and "Mandy's Hand Jive."

Lois LaFond

Boulder-based vocalist Lois LaFond began recording music for young listeners when she couldn't find appropriate music for her own children. By striving to create music for children that respects their individuality, acknowledges their growing sophistication, and builds self-esteem, she has developed into an innovative writer, performer, and producer of music for family audiences. Remarkably refined and complex in sound and content, Lois's recordings are also just plain fun.

Currently the lead vocalist with an eighteen-piece jazz band and a twelve-piece African-pop band in Boulder, both adult-focused, Lois has assembled her own five-piece band, the Rockadiles, to bring multicultural, contemporary sounds to children. Her music, which has been called "uncluttered and refreshing" by New Age pianist George Winston, has been used successfully with learning-disabled as well as gifted children.

In addition to the recordings listed below, Lois LaFond has recorded *While Creatures of Summer Sleep,* a collection of stories and songs designed to highlight major events during the school year.

I Am Who I Am (1985)
Boulder Children's Productions
P.O. Box 4712
Boulder, CO 80306
Format: Cassette
Age Appeal: All ages
Target Ages: 2–5
Material: Sophisticated songs of self-esteem, self-awareness, and imagination for very young listeners; songs introduced by children; lyrics included
Vocals: Lois LaFond with children's chorus
Vocal Style: Clear, expressive, tuneful

Instrumentation: Drums, percussion, pedal steel guitar, congas, bass, saxophone, trumpet

Using a rich variety of musical styles, including rock, jazz, salsa, reggae, and African rhythms, *I Am Who I Am* is a multileveled collection of songs for preschoolers and their families. Many of the lyrics have been created by children. Some songs have choruses in French and Spanish.

   Song highlights include "I Am Who I Am," "Space Is Going to Be Fun," "My Room," and "Living Things."

Something New (1987)

Boulder Children's Productions
Format: Cassette
Age Appeal: Newborn to toddler
Material: Original and traditional music from around the world
Vocals: Lois LaFond and friends
Vocal Style: Rich and soothing
Instrumentation: Harp, violins, piano, Osi drums, flute

Included on *Something New* are a nineteenth-century Scottish lullaby and a Sioux Indian chant. Several of the selections are instrumental. Side 2 contains twenty minutes of heartbeat enhanced by drums and additional percussion.

One World (1989)

Boulder Children's Productions
Format: Cassette
Age Appeal: All ages
Target Ages: 5–9
Material: Rich, energetic songs about humanity, imagination, and self-esteem; lyrics sheet included
Vocals: Lois LaFond with Carlton Bacon and children's chorus
Vocal Style: Crisp, uncluttered, delicately expressive, and tuneful
Instrumentation: Performed by the Rockadiles and Orchestra King Mama, an Afro-Caribbean pop band, using drums, percussion, congas, bongos, bells, triangle, shakers, guitars, pedal steel guitar, bass, saxophone, clarinet, trumpet

If you are a fan of the Afro-pop sound made popular in the United States by Paul Simon's *Graceland,* you will adore listening to Lois LaFond's *One World* with your children. Lois's graceful voice weaves in and out of the rich, compelling music. The lyrics, many of which are direct quotes from Lois's own two children, deal with feelings and observations. They are elegant and (unlike many of the tunes on *Graceland*) easy to understand. The end result is a fun, multileveled album.

Song highlights include "Part of the Family," an enegetic, uplifting song about our family of neighbors all around the globe, with a chorus in French, Russian, Spanish, and Japanese; "I Lost My Shoes," a blues lament with a happy ending; "Some Days Are Happier than Others," a song of acceptance performed a capella with haunting harmonies; "Smile," with an exuberant South African sound, which promotes the power of smiling; "In Control," with a reggae beat, which urges kids to take control of the pictures in their minds to help themselves overcome fears; and "One World," a call-and-response song that celebrates global unity, with verses in French, Japanese, Russian, Chinese, and Spanish.

Francine Lancaster

An opera singer and former editor at *Cosmopolitan* magazine, Francine Lancaster founded Lancaster Productions in 1984 because she could not find recorded classics of children's music to play for her own son. Believing that other parents of her generation—in their late thirties and early forties—would be interested in fun and challenging children's music, Francine hired first-rate musicians and a superb arranger (her husband, James Shallenberger) and employed up-to-the-minute recording techniques to enhance her clear, silky, operatic voice.

Working with illustrator and concerned mother Anya Horvath, whom she met in the course of giving a music program for toddlers, Francine packaged her delightful first recording with innovation and pizazz. *Nursery Songs and Lullabies,* enclosed in an appealing "keepsake" gift box with a charmingly illustrated forty-page songbook, sold out its first edition of ten thousand copies within six months.

In response to the overwhelming success of her first musical production, Francine has gone on to create several more titles in the same delightful boxed cassette-book format. While each has its own specific musical thematic focus, by far the most visually beautiful of the Lancaster packages is *Mother Goose and Other Nursery Songs,* which Francine produced in conjunction with the Boston Museum of Fine Arts, using stunning, historic illustrations by Walter Crane and Randolph Caldecott from the museum's collection.

Francine Sings a Keepsake of Nursery Songs and Lullabies (1984)

Lancaster Productions
P.O. Box 7820
Berkeley, CA 94707-0820
Format: Cassette
Age Appeal: Newborn–5
Material: Traditional songs; songbook with illustrations by Anya Horvath
Vocals: Francine Lancaster
Vocal Style: Classical soprano
Instrumentation: Orchestra

Among the more than twenty-five selections, highlights include "Frère Jacques," "The Mulberry Bush," "This Old Man," "Pop Goes the Weasel," "Hey Diddle Diddle," "Old King Cole," "Mary Had a Little Lamb," "Itsy Bitsy Spider," "Row, Row, Row Your Boat," "Twinkle, Twinkle Little Star," "Hush, Little Baby," "All the Pretty Little Horses," "All Through the Night," and Brahms's "Lullaby."

Francine Sings a Keepsake of Favorite Animal Songs (1985)

Lancaster Productions
Format: Cassette
(See *Francine Sings a Keepsake of Nursery Songs and Lullabies* above for details.)

Among the more than twenty songs, highlights include "Hickory, Dickery, Dock," "I Love Little Pussy," "Polly Parakeet," "Oh Where, Oh Where Has My Little Dog Gone?," "Old MacDonald Had a Farm," "Bingo," "The Little White Duck," "All the Fish Are Swimming," "Cuckoo, Cuckoo, Calls From the Wood," "The Bear Went Over the Mountain."

Francine Sings a Keepsake of Favorite Holiday Songs (1986)

Lancaster Productions
Format: Cassette
Age Appeal: All ages
Material: Traditional songs of Thanksgiving, Chanukah, Christmas, and New Year's; songbook with illustrations by Patrick Kroboth
Vocals: Francine Lancaster
Vocal Style: Classical soprano
Instrumentation: Orchestra

Song highlights include "Over the River," "We Gather Together," "O Hanukkah," "My Dreydl," "The Latke Song," "Jingle Bells," "Deck the Halls," "Christmas Eve Round," "Away in a Manger," "Silent Night," and "The Old Year Now Away Is Fled (Greensleeves)."

Francine Sings a Keepsake of Mother Goose and Other Nursery Songs (1987)

Lancaster Productions
Format: Cassette
(See *Francine Sings a Keepsake of Nursery Songs and Lullabies*, page 125, for details.)

Memorabilia buffs will be attracted to this enchanting package and songbook assembled from historic Crane and Caldecott artwork owned by the Museum of Fine Arts in Boston.

Highlights among the more than twenty songs include "Hey Diddle Diddle," "The Three Little Kittens," "Baa! Baa! Black Sheep," "Tom, the Piper's Son," "Song of Sixpence," "The Mulberry Bush," "Little Jack Horner," "Hot Cross Buns," and "Aiken Drum."

Gary Lapow

When it comes to creating positive, humorous music with gentle yet authentic rock sounds, Gary Lapow has a magic touch. His recordings will appeal to savvy young listeners and their parents.

Gary, whose smoky voice is occasionally reminiscent of Paul Simon's, spent years as a singer of folk-based adult songs, performing with the Freedom Singers and Malvina Reynolds. He discovered his talent for children's music when he co-directed the Cazadero Family Camp with his (now) wife Ahbi Vernon, and these days he spends his time working exclusively with children. Having developed a curriculum at the Wolf Trap Institute for Early Learning Through the Performing Arts in Virginia, he teaches in Head Start programs (some of the songs on his most recent recording come from these experiences), performs in schools in the San Francisco Bay area, and participates in children's music festivals throughout the country and in Canada. Gary Lapow also appears in concert on the Disney Channel.

A spokesperson for the Vancouver Children's Festival has described Gary Lapow as "many things rolled into one. This includes writing, singing and playing wonderfully inventive songs for children. Gary's approach is soft, relaxed, witty and never ever patronizing."

Sing a Silly Song (1984)

Springboard Records
2140 Shattuck Ave.
P.O. Box 2317
Berkeley, CA 94704
Format: Cassette
Target Ages: 3–5
Material: Witty, inventive songs (many by Gary Lapow) of fantasy, friendship, and humanity, with a contemporary soft-rock sound; lyrics included
Vocals: Gary Lapow with backup vocals
Vocal Style: Enthusiastic, tuneful pop sound
Instrumentation: Guitars, keyboard

Highlights of this gentle recording include "Magic Penny," "I Can't Sleep," "Rainy Day," "A Little Bit of L-O-V-E," "Sing a Silly Song," "You're My Friend," "Song About Feet," and "Fleas."

Supermarket Shuffle (1985)

Springboard Records
Format: Cassette
Target Ages: 4–7
Material: Witty, inventive songs (many by Gary Lapow) of fantasy, friendship, and humanity, with a contemporary soft-rock sound; lyrics included
Vocals: Gary Lapow with backup vocals by Dan Goldensohn and the Goldensohn Gate Quartet Trio
Vocal Style: Enthusiastic, tuneful pop sound
Instrumentation: Guitars, keyboards, synthesized bass, accordion, harmonica, bells, and whistles

Highlights of this engaging recording include "Supermarket Shuffle," "Give and Take," "My Aunt Came Back," "The Bread Song," "Chatty Chatty," "My Kitty Cat."

I Like Noodles (1987)
Springboard Records
Format: Cassette
Age Appeal: 2–5
(See *Supermarket Shuffle*, page 127, for musical details.)

Song highlights include "I Like Noodles," "Talking on the Telephone," "Drums on Daddy's Tummy," "Apples and Bananas," "Peace," "Hello Hello," "Numbers Rap," and "Choo Choo Train."

John McCutcheon

Who is John McCutcheon? you might ask. In the words of Pete Seeger, he is "not only one of the best musicians in the U.S.A., expert on the hammered dulcimer, fiddle, and a half-dozen other instruments, but also a great singer, songwriter, and song leader."

How lucky we are that McCutcheon became a father. In addition to performing and recording for adult audiences, this virtuoso musician has become involved in creating music for family listening.

John's warm, affecting voice and superb musicianship are linked to tradition, yet his sensibility is focused clearly on the present. On two superb children's recordings of his own and on several others in which he has been involved (including *The Kids of Widney High*), his musical skills have meshed with his innate concern for humanity, resulting in recordings that consistently inspire and entertain.

If your idea of family fun is to listen with your children to humorous, humane, exuberant music (as it is mine), get hold of John McCutcheon's award-winning recordings listed below. Both come with illustrated songbooks for coloring. (It's really relaxing to color while you're listening to music, though it's sometimes hard to sit still while McCutcheon music fills the airwaves.)

John also publishes a newsletter in which he reports about his recordings, his performance schedule, his family, and his thoughts on the state of the world. To receive a copy, write to Appalseed Productions, 1025 Locust Avenue, Charlottesville, Virginia 22901.

Howjadoo (1983)
Rounder Records
1 Camp St.
Cambridge, MA 02140
Format: Cassette, LP
Age Appeal: All ages
Target Ages: 3–8
Material: Traditional and contemporary songs that promote imagination and humanity
Vocals: John McCutcheon with backup by adults and children
Vocal Style: Exuberant, folk based
Instrumentation: Guitar, banjo, hammered dulcimer, fiddle, Autoharp, jaw harp, spoons, viola, bass, cello, piano, tuba, tin whistle, drums, harmonica, ocarina, bells, triangle, Cajun accordion

On *Howjadoo* John McCutcheon eloquently blends superb traditional sounds with contemporary sensitivity. Humor, humanity, and toe-tapping music effortlessly interweave to make fulfilling listening for a wide age range of children and adults.

Of special note in this award-winning collection of songs are "Cut the Cake," a celebration of birthdays for people of all ages; "Howjadoo," which encourages people to greet each other; "Molly and the Whale," in which Molly, despite her skeptical father, gets to know a whale; "Rubber Blubber Whale," a silly and incredibly catchy song; "Peanut Butter," a traditional and very funny recounting of how to get peanut butter off one's tongue; "Babysitter," in which a child airs his displeasure at being left behind; "Father Grumble," who tries to take on his wife's chores and gains a new respect for her skills; and a warm and comforting "Tender Shepherd."

Mail Myself to You (1988)
Rounder Records
Format: Cassette, LP
Age Appeal: All ages
Target Ages: 3–8
Material: Traditional and contemporary songs that celebrate animals and people
Vocals: John McCutcheon with harmony vocals and children's chorus
Vocal Style: Full, appealing, folk based

Instrumentation: Acoustic and electric guitars, banjo, hammered dulcimers, fiddle, Autoharp, jaw harp, hambone, trumpet, piano, harmonica, drums and percussion, trumpet, saxophones, clarinet, and synthesizer

His skills honed in traditional folk music, with *Mail Myself to You* John McCutcheon has taken a major step into a full, contemporary sound. Whether rock 'n' roll, jazz, mountain music, juba, or calypso, his exquisite music is tremendous fun.

John has assembled material with care and sensitivity. As with *Howjadoo,* there is a lot to hear, sing, and celebrate. Special advice: Do not play this rousing recording before bedtime!

Highlights include "Over in the Meadow," a traditional song that never sounded more relevant and contemporary as John describes habitats and habits in the animal world rock 'n' roll style; Woody Guthrie's "Mail Myself to You," with its playful imagery; "The Awful Hilly Daddy-Willie Trip," in which young Will McCutcheon has to endure an endless car ride with his dad; "The Kindergarten Wall," describing the lessons of kindergarten as lessons to remember for all time; and "Turn Around," Malvina Reynolds's moving song about the passage of childhood.

Bob McGrath

While Bob McGrath will be a familiar name for viewers of "Sesame Street," parents may not know about his delightful independent recordings for very young listeners. With his friendly tenor voice he sings gentle, spirited children's classics. Kept purposefully simple, his lovely recordings are thoughtful choices for youngest listeners.

The Baby Record (1985)
Golden Music
Western Publishing
1220 Mound Ave.
Racine, WI 53404
Format: Cassette, LP
Age Appeal: Newborn–2 years
Material: Forty traditional rhymes, songs, and games with narrative how-to instructions for parents
Vocals: Bob McGrath and Katharine Smithrim

Vocal Style: Expressive, clear, gentle narration and singing

Instrumentation: Primarily a capella with some simple drums, shakers, and bells

Looking for a great baby gift? Try *The Baby Record*. Bob McGrath and Katharine Smithrim are enthusiastic, articulate hosts as they move parent and infant through a series of simple activities. Adapting Katharine's "Music with Your Baby" classes, each side contains gentle tunes organized in the following areas: bouncing rhymes; finger and toe plays; action rhymes; instrument play with drums, shakers, and bells; and lullabies. Some of the songs included are "Ride Baby Ride," "To Market, To Market," "Round and Round the Garden," "These Are Baby's Fingers," "Baby's on My Knee," and "Jack Be Nimble."

Songs and Games for Toddlers (1985)

Golden Music

Format: Cassette, LP

Age Appeal: 18 months–3 years

Material: Rhythms, songs, and games and how-to instructions that are geared to toddlers and their care givers

Vocals: Bob McGrath and Katharine Smithrim

Vocal Style: Expressive, clear, gentle narration and singing

Instrumentation: Primarily a capella, with percussion accompaniments by Bill Usher

Activity songs and games to be shared by a toddler and an adult are appealingly presented here by Bob McGrath and Katharine Smithrim. Clearly a "hands on" recording, the gentle, age-targeted material is meant to encourage musical dialogue between parents and toddlers both as the music plays and later, as they share their lives away from the recording. The album contains more than thirty songs, including "Your Name Is," "Rig a Jig Jig," "We're Going to Kentucky," "Walk When the Drum Says Walk," "It's Raining, It's Pouring," "Rain, Rain, Go Away," "This Old Man," and "Row, Row, Row Your Boat."

If You're Happy and You Know It Sing with Bob,
Volumes 1 and 2 (1985)

Golden Music

Format: Cassette, LP

Age Appeal: 2–4

Material: Children's standards

Vocals: Bob McGrath

Vocal Style: Clear, crisp, tuneful pop
Instrumentation: Piano, guitar, banjo, percussion, xylophone, woodwinds, strings, horns

Each volume contains more than thirty singable songs. Highlights of Volume 1 include "If You're Happy and You Know It," "The Wheels on the Bus," "Five Little Monkeys," "Willoughby Wallaby Woo," "When the Saints Go Marching In," "A Little Wheel Turnin'," "Mr. Sun," "Where Is Thumkin?," "This Little Light of Mine."

Highlights of Volume 2 include "Who Built the Ark?," "Three Blind Mice," "Old King Cole," "The Hokey Pokey," "Let Everyone Clap Hands Like Me," "I've Been Working on the Railroad," "You'll Sing a Song," "Bingo," "John Jacob Jingleheimer Schmidt," and "We've Got the Whole World in Our Hands."

Marcy Marxer

Having spent many years testing and perfecting her music in classrooms and in conference and concert halls, Marcy Marxer has become a regular artist at the Wolf Trap Institute for Early Learning Through the Performing Arts. In January 1987 she presented a series of "Jump Children" programs for the Smithsonian Institution in Washington, and the results have come together as the delightful, high-energy recording *Jump Children*.

Jump Children (1986)
Rounder Records
1 Camp St.
Cambridge, MA 02140
Format: Cassette, LP, CD
Age Appeal: 2–9
Material: Traditional and 1940s revivals; activity book available
Vocals: Marcy Marxer and friends
Vocal Style: Clear, commanding folk voice, with energetic, rousing harmonies
Instrumentation: Mandolin, dulcimer, fiddle, guitar, piano, horns, clarinet

Jump Children is an unusual, upbeat collection of songs and sounds that is sophisticated enough to appeal to hard-to-please six- to nine-year-olds and skeptical parents but is also appropriate for two- to four-year-old listeners. This is the kind of music parents can play during a car trip and make everybody happy.

Marcy Marxer has a distinctive and compelling voice that bounces effortlessly between sounds of the swing era and more traditional folk music. To create this rich, delightfully focused musical atmosphere, Marcy Marxer has gathered more than twenty musical friends to back her up, among them the multitalented Cathy Fink.

"Jump Children," "Rock-a-Bye Boogie," and "Chickery Chick" all swing with the refreshing energy of the big band sound; "Beautiful Day" moves with a gentle calypso beat, while "Hush, Little Baby" has a reggae rhythm. Marcy Marxer's musical skill comes shining through as she and her friends join together with their mandolin, dulcimer, fiddle, and banjo to create a wonderful string-band version of the traditional "Grandpa's Farm."

The annotated, illustrated activity book that is available from Marcy for a small fee is a wonderful companion to "Jump Children." It contains words, dance steps, and hand signals to the songs on the album as well as instructions for how to make rhythm instruments. Also included is a chart showing parents and teachers which songs and movements enhance development of gross motor control, teach body parts, and introduce American sign language.

Mary Miché

The oldest of six children, Mary Miché was inspired by her mother's magical ability to create peace in the family car by getting everyone to sing together. While Mary's sisters are now architects and engineers, Mary has made a career of training teachers to bring music into their classrooms, performing for children, and directing children's choruses. In her spare time she sings choral music with adults and works as a licensed therapist.

Mary Miché has a passion for collecting great songs for kids. To this end she has created several theme-oriented recordings filled with imaginative old and new tunes. She has selected songs from the best of today's innovative writers, including Shel Silverstein, Barry Louis Polisar, Gary Lapow, and John McCutcheon, and has written a few herself. Perfect for home and car listening, Mary's recordings are also ideal for teachers who want to enhance science and language arts experiences in the classroom.

In compiling her collections, Mary has had two important goals. She wants her recordings to stimulate children to sing along simply for the pleasure of it, and she wants to make learning fun. In both, she succeeds beautifully. The songs are humorous and catchy and use sophisticated, imaginative vocabulary. Mary's delightful voice is clear, and so perfectly pitched in the right range for children (and many adults) that it's a real pleasure to listen and sing along. She presents facts and concepts with so much good humor that it will be hard for a child to associate the experience with learning.

Mary's tapes are available through catalogues and children's bookstores and directly from her. Because Mary has such strong feelings about children having the opportunity to hear and sing quality music, she has thought of some clever ways for schools, nature centers, and other needy child-centered organizations to finance music programs. Feel free to contact her at the Song Trek address below.

Additional titles by Mary Miché are *Kids' Stuff* and *Peace It Together*.

Earthy Tunes (1987)
Song Trek
2600 Hillegass
Berkeley, CA 94704
Format: Cassette
Age Appeal: 3–11
Target Ages: 7–8
Material: Traditional and contemporary songs about plants, animals, and bugs
Vocals: Mary Miché
Vocal Style: Light and lyric, with clear diction
Instrumentation: Guitar, mandolin, banjo, jaw harp, fiddle

Earthy Tunes, available in many national park gift shops, is a perfect cassette to buy and play while on a family trip to the woods. To round out your outdoor experience, play it in your cabin or tent in the evening, or while traveling home in the car. In addition to giving you new attitudes and facts about many of the creatures you meet in the wild, singing along with Mary is so much fun for everyone that it will help your family outing shine in your collective memory.

Among the nearly twenty songs, highlights include "Animal Party," "Spiders and Snakes," "Banana Slug Song," "Dirt Made My Lunch," "Bugs in Your Bark," "What Is a Tree?," and "Lotta Seeds Grow."

Holly Daze (1988)
Song Trek
Format: Cassette
Age Appeal: 3–11
Target Ages: 7–8
Material: Traditional and contemporary songs that celebrate fall and winter, Halloween, Thanksgiving, Christmas, the New Year, and Martin Luther King Day
Vocals: Mary Miché
Instrumentation: Guitar, banjo, keyboards, drums

Sensitive to music that brightens and intensifies holiday celebrations for children, Mary Miché has assembled a sparkling collection of traditional and contemporary songs. Intended to help kids and adults celebrate secular and religious holidays as well as the changing seasons, this tape can be well utilized in an elementary-grade classroom or in a family car cassette player.

Highlights include "The Haunted House," "The Boogie-Woogie Ghost," "Snowflakes in My Ear," "The Thanksgiving Song," "Hava Nashira," "The Christmas Mouse," "Jingle Bell Rock," and "The Dream of Martin Luther King."

Eric Nagler

Back in the 1960s people gathered around the fountain in New York's Washington Square Park on Sundays to make music together. Eric Nagler, fourteen years old, was there with his banjo. In 1968, after college, Eric moved to Canada, where he put aside work on his Ph.D. in psychology, opened the Toronto Folklore Centre, the first center of its kind in Canada, and began to perform as a studio musician.

Eric was introduced to the idea of family audiences in 1978, when old friends Rick Avery and Judy Greenhill gave their "homemade music" program at the library in his town. Afterwards they invited Eric to take over their circuit—and he did.

Soon Eric was playing backups on recordings made by Sharon, Lois and Bram, becoming a featured performer on their successful television series, "The Elephant Show." He has gone on to create a television special of his own, "The Eric Nagler Generic Holiday Family Music Special for All Seasons," as well as a variety of video and book projects, including his recently published book *Any Fool Can Do It*. Containing anecdotes about his lifelong love of music making as well as simple instructions for making homemade instruments, it is, like his music, for people of all ages.

Maintaining a hectic performance schedule throughout North America, Eric continues to give hundreds of family concerts, during which he encourages every member of the audience to have fun making music. To call an Eric Nagler performance "high energy" is an understatement. A master of more than a dozen instruments, including the mandolin, guitar, and fiddle, Eric delights in helping people make music, dispensing spoons, kazoos, and assorted unconventional instruments to his enthusiastic audience. No concert is complete without inspired performances on washtubs, bleach bottles, and Eric's own zany creation, the sewerphone. He is determined to get everyone playing, clapping, and singing. The results are phenomenal.

Recently Eric has added another innovative dimension to his performance repertoire. Featuring his homemade instruments against a backdrop of a conventional orchestra, the "Symphony Show" includes a duel between the tuba player and Eric on the infamous sewerphone.

"I like to think I provide entertainment that adults and kids can enjoy together," he explains. "All too often music can separate us. It should bring us together."

It's hardly a surprise that Eric has produced several superb recordings for family listening—spirited and sassy, with an intergenerational "music hall" sound. Eric's impeccable vocals and musicianship and his choice of ageless standards and original material combine to make rich and rewarding family recordings.

In addition to the recordings described below, Eric has recorded *Fiddle Up a Tune* on Elephant Records.

Come On In (1985)

Elephant Records
P.O. Box 101, Station Z
Toronto, Ontario, Canada M5N 2Z3
Format: Cassette, LP
Age Appeal: All ages
Target Ages: 5–8
Material: Old standards and original songs performed with folk, jazz and swing, and jug band influences; lyrics included
Vocals: Eric Nagler
Vocal Style: Robust, tuneful, folk based

Instrumentation: Banjo, mandolin, fiddle, Jew's harp, saxophone, trumpet, kazoo, psaltery, spoons, sewerphone

Highlights of this rich, energetic album are "Come On In!," "Boom Boom, Ain't It Great to Be Crazy?," "Button Up Your Overcoat," "My Lovely Sewerphone," "Be Kind to Your Parents," "Friendship Pin," and "Don't Say Goodbye."

Improvise with Eric Nagler (1989)

Rounder Records
1 Camp Street
Cambridge, MA 02140
Format: Cassette, LP
Age Appeal: All ages
Target Ages: 5–8
Material: Eclectic, including standards, contemporary compositions, and original songs performed with folk, jazz and swing, and jug band influences; lyrics included
Vocals: Eric Nagler with Christopher Nagler and backup by adults and children
Vocal Style: Robust, tuneful, folk based
Instrumentation: Banjo, mandolin, fiddle, Jew's harp, washboard, saxophone, clarinet, harmonica, accordion, trumpet, trombone, tuba, kazoo, psaltery, spoons, sewerphone, guitar, percussion, keyboards

With his remarkable flair for the zany, Eric Nagler has created a superb, fun-filled recording. Highlights of *Improvise with Eric Nagler* include "Mairzy Doats," with its classic word play; "Just Not Fair," which presents the inequities of being a kid; "I'll Give You Fair," which is Eric's amusing reply; "Dueling Tubas," in which Eric takes on the musical battle with his wonderful sewerphone; "The Strangest Dream," Ed McCurdy's 1950 masterpiece about making peace, with lead vocals sung movingly by young Christopher Nagler and backup by Eric with the Walton Memorial Church Family Chorus; "The Body Song," in which Eric can't resist the opportunity to have fun with the English language; and "Super Mom," in which kids learn that other people's jobs are not as easy as they may look.

Tim Noah

Endearing and talented Tim Noah, who has been involved with Tickle Tune Typhoon as member and contributor, now creates strong and unique material for children as a solo performer.

In addition to the recording listed below, he has released *Kaddywompas* in 1989, which contains songs with a country-and-western flavor.

In Search of the Wow Wow Wibble Woggle Wazzie Woodle Woo! (1983)

Noazart Productions
P.O. Box 30501
Seattle, WA 98103
Format: Cassette, LP
Age Appeal: All ages
Target Ages: 5–9
Material: Exuberant rock opera
Vocals: Tim Noah with elaborate backup vocals by children and adults
Vocal Style: Folk-rock
Instrumentation: Guitars, keyboards, drums, saxophone, percussion, harmonica

This recording and its companion video have been given awards many times over, and for good reason. Charismatic Tim Noah makes high-powered music that surges through the airways, bubbling with full sounds that evoke memories of the Beatles' *Sgt. Pepper's Lonely Hearts Club Band.* Children and adults who have trouble appreciating laid-back folk-oriented recordings will have no such problems here. To go in search of the Wow Wow Wibble Woggle Wazzie Woodle Woo, listeners must buy into a thinly structured story which turns out to be irresistible as audio cues and commanding music herald the beginning of Tim Noah's fantastic adventure. While the video version sets the stage visually, in our house we became addicted to this graphic, energetic audio recording well before we got a glimpse of the inventive video.

Songs include "Zoom," which sets the energetic tone for the album with a happy blast-off into outer space; "If I Only Knew," in which Tim admits to the kids on board the rocket ship that he doesn't know much about the object of their search (no one minds); "If I Was," set in a jungle, where Tim sings about the habits of possum, bird, snake, elephant, and rhino; "The Monkey Song," about self-determination, in which Tim sings, "I want to do just what I please / And build a house up in the trees"; "Big Booger," in which Tim cries to his teacher for protection from a bully; "Tears on My Toes," a short song about the frustrations of not being able to find the Wazzie Woodle; "Little Miracles," sung by a magician to describe his craft; "Sunshiney Mornin'," a toe tapper in celebration of a great new beginning; "Musty Moldy Melvin," in which Tim sings about a host of creepy yet humorous characters who live in a mucky swamp; "Friends with a Song," a moving ode to friendship in which Tim sings his heart out (after a few listens, you find yourself singing along too); "I Can Do Anything," a touching song of empowerment which reminds this listener that if children are to realize their dreams, they must feel good about themselves.

Hap Palmer

Having written and recorded more than two hundred songs, Hap Palmer is surely America's most prolific children's songwriter. Trained as an early-childhood educator, Palmer began his writing and performing career in 1969, when he created *Learning Basic Skills Through Music* to use in his own classroom. More than thirty recordings have followed, marketed primarily to educators—until recently only teachers and their lucky students enjoyed the work of Hap Palmer.

While many Hap Palmer recordings stress classroom skills, including movement, rhythm, vocabulary, and math development, Hap Palmer has also created albums that are ideal for home listening. Focusing on early-childhood and elementary-age issues and themes, he is as much on target with the five-to-nine-year-old sensibility as he is with the two-to-four-year-old stage of development.

Palmer's innovative, award-winning recordings, as well as the books and videotapes that have grown from them, are becoming easier to find in catalogues and in book and record stores. But every Hap Palmer creation is targeted to a specific age and purpose, so choose with care. For more information on recordings by Hap Palmer, write to Educational Activities at the address below.

Babysong (1984)
Educational Activities, Inc.
P.O. Box 392
Freeport, NY 11520
Format: Cassette, LP

Age Appeal: 2–4
Material: Original songs about the experiences of a toddler
Vocals: Hap Palmer
Vocal Style: Gentle folk-pop
Instrumentation: Electric keyboard and synthesizer

Babysong is a real standout for nursery-age listeners. Hap and Martha Palmer have put together catchy phrasing and pop-oriented arrangements to create touching, disarming songs about many of the experiences of early childhood. If your child is about to turn two or three, or if there is a holiday in the near future, be sure to put this recording on your gift list. If there's no official reason to celebrate just around the corner, proclaim an *All Ears* family celebration of your own.

Hap Palmer sings in such a gentle, warm style that you will be surprised at how directly he deals with powerful topics. His titles tell part of the story: "My Mommy Comes Back," "Today I Took My Diapers Off," "I Sleep 'til the Morning." All are songs of reassurance and affirmation: Mommy *will* come back; it's hard to learn to share toys, but it's worth the effort; it feels good to remember learning to walk; no one likes to have his or her security blanket washed; and (remarkably) it's exciting to learn to use the potty.

"Come Read a Book" contains references to children's book classics, including *Green Eggs and Ham, The Little Engine That Could, Good Night Moon,* and *Peter Rabbit.* If you and your child are familiar with these classics, the song will be even more effective, so plan a trip to the library for copies of any of the titles that your child has yet to meet.

"Sittin' in a High Chair," written to the tune of the traditional "Mammy's Little Baby Loves Shortenin' Bread," is a rousing anthem to babies' distinct way of eating. It's sure to lighten parents' dread of yet another messy meal.

Backwards Land (1987)

Hap-Pal Music, Inc.
P.O. Box 323
Topanga, CA 90290
Format: Cassette, LP
Age Appeal: 5–8
Material: Thoughtful and humorous songs about children's issues, concerns, and values
Vocals: Hap Palmer

Vocal Style: Gentle, eclectic sound, including folk, rock, and jazz influences
Instrumentation: Guitars, flute, saxophone, keyboard synthesizer, percussion

At first listen, the comfortable folk-pop resonance of Hap Palmer's voice, the cheerful children's chorus, and the light synthesizer backups combine to make *Backwards Land* a suspiciously sweet-sounding album. But don't be fooled. The tunes are catchy and singable, and the lyrics, which tackle important issues for early-elementary-age children, can pack a big wallop.

Hap Palmer is a gifted wordsmith who has created songs that entertain but can also, for those who want to go the next step, open paths of communication between teacher and student or parent and child. They cover a broad range of topics and emotions—there's something here for everyone.

Highlights include "Backwards Land," reminiscent of Lerner and Loewe's "Camelot," describing a whimsical place where children can revel in the reordering of priorities; "When Things Don't Go Your Way," detailing many of the frustrations and inequalities of childhood as well as how different children deal with them, with the message that it's okay to find your own solutions; and "Amanda Schlupp," complete with a *Sgt. Pepper*–like keyboard accompaniment—the kind of song that will make every parent smile and every child shudder as it paints a vivid vision of the classic messy room.

One of my all-time favorite songs is the tongue-in-cheek "Helping Mommy in the Kitchen." Presenting the opposite side of the "Amanda Schlupp" situation, it gives equal time to kids. Again, kids who pick up on the lyrics will roar at Hap Palmer's images. But this time, finicky parents will blanch as the song describes children who demolish the kitchen in the guise of lending a hand.

Tom Paxton

If you are just to one side or the other of forty, you may remember singer-songwriter Tom Paxton from the sixties, because he wrote many songs that have since become standards. "Ramblin' Boy," "I Can't Help But Wonder," "The Last Thing on My Mind" are a few of the titles of songs he's written for adult listening. John Denver has said of Tom, "In my opinion, he's the greatest songwriter in the world, and someday I hope to do an album of Tom's songs."

What you may not realize is that Tom is also the author of several classic children's songs. "The Marvellous Toy" and "Going to the Zoo" are among them.

Where's Tom Paxton now? you might wonder. He's right where he's always been—writing songs, making recordings, and giving concerts around the world. Since one of his favorite stateside venues is the Intermedia Art Center, a treasure of a concert space that's in Huntington, New York, near where I live, I can reliably report that Tom's music continues to be politically relevant and appropriately humorous or moving. His tuneful voice remains clear and compelling.

Also the proud user of a Macintosh computer, Tom produces a seasonal newsletter describing his newest recordings and publishing projects as well as his performance itinerary. He will be delighted to put you on his mailing list if you drop him a line at PAX Records, 78 Park Place, East Hampton, New York 11937. In addition to the recording listed below, Tom also released for children *Balloon-Aloon-Aloon* in 1987 on his PAX label.

The Marvellous Toy and Other Gallimaufry (1984)

Flying Fish Records
1304 W. Schubert
Chicago, IL 60614
Format: Cassette, LP
Age Appeal: 3–5
Material: Original songs about childhood
Vocals: Tom Paxton
Vocal Style: Clear, tuneful folk
Instrumentation: Guitar

Highlights include "Jennifer's Rabbit," "The Marvellous Toy," "Come and Play Catch with Me," "Hush-You-Bye, Go to Sleep," "Going to the Zoo," "The Thought Stayed Free," "My Dog's Bigger Than Your Dog," and "Let's Pretend."

Sarah Pirtle

An award-winning novelist, Sarah Pirtle is an active advocate for networking among children's music artists.

Two Hands Hold the Earth (1984)

A Gentle Wind
P.O. Box 3103
Albany, NY 12203

Target Ages: 4–7
Material: Gentle, intelligent, original songs of imagination, nature, and humanity
Vocals: Sarah Pirtle with backup
Vocal Style: Warm, folk influenced
Instrumentation: Guitar, banjo, flute

Highlights of this humane, environmentally focused recording include the graceful and soaring "The Magic Horse"; "Pelorus Jack," about a faithful and friendly dolphin who is threatened by a sniper; "There's Always Something You Can Do," which offers techniques for dealing with anger; "My Roots Go Down"; "Wish I Was a Whale"; "Jump, Salmon, Jump"; and "Two Hands Hold the Earth."

Also by Sarah Pirtle on A Gentle Wind: *The Wind Is Telling Secrets.*

David Polansky

Animal Alphabet Songs (1982)
Perfect Score
P.O. Box 61
Cochituate, MA 01778
Format: Cassette
Age Appeal: All ages
Target Ages: 3–5
Material: A witty, sophisticated, singing sampler of animals
Vocals: David Polansky and friends
Vocal Style: Ingratiating, tuneful cabaret-variety
Instrumentation: Piano, trumpet, synthesizer

David Polansky has combined witty lyrics, rhythms, instrumentation, and colorful vocal delivery to create fast-moving vignettes depicting animals. Humorous and sophisticated, this recording provides rich listening for adults as well as young children. Animals included are alligator, bear, camel, duck, elephant, fox, giraffe, hippopotamus, iguana, jaguar, kangaroo, lion, monkey, narwhal, octopus, porcupine, quahog, rabbit, skunk, turtle, uakari, vicuna, whale, "x" animals, yak, and zebra.

I Like Dessert (1987)
Perfect Score
Format: Cassette
Age Appeal: All ages
Target Ages: 5–8
Material: Original songs celebrating the joys and struggles of the early-elementary years
Vocals: David Polansky and children's chorus
Vocal Style: Ingratiating, tuneful cabaret
Instrumentation: Piano, trumpet, synthesizer

I Like Dessert is an upbeat look at life in elementary school, written and performed with charm and energy by singer-pianist David Polansky, whose style is occasionally reminiscent of Tom Lehrer's.

Highlights include "Another Day at School," "Ben Hem Boogie," "The Gurgles," "Bo Yabba Dee Bah," "I Like Dessert," and "Talk It Out."

Barry Louis Polisar

Barry Louis Polisar is an American treasure. The innovative, bad-boy attitude of his tell-it-like-it-is songs has altered forever the way children and adults can communicate through music. Bordering on the disrespectful, liberally laced with rude noises, sometimes sung off-key, his songs may upset you if you are easily offended. But Barry is irresistible to kids, who have long needed a determined and articulate spokesperson to remind the world of childhood's realities. If you want to talk to the children in your family or classroom about things that matter to them, you'll find the challenge easier and a lot more fun if you listen together to Barry Louis Polisar.

Back in the dark ages of 1974, music for children was dismissed as unprofitable by members of the business world. Barry, with a stubbornness and naivete that might be considered "childlike," refused to be put off. He produced and distributed his first recording himself, and then did the same with another, and another, and another. At this writing, Barry has created for his own label eight original albums, six books, and two videotapes and is performing constantly for families and schools.

Barry Louis Polisar has received rave reviews from newspapers and magazines all over the country, including *Gifted and Talented Magazine,* which said: "Songs of Barry Louis Polisar . . . appeal to a wide audience of children and adults who still think like children. . . . Polisar explores sensitive areas where the poetry and fun of a song are more expressive than prose." The *Times Dispatch* of Richmond, Virginia, has said: "Polisar's songs examine children's hidden thoughts and feelings, tackling previously taboo subjects in an honest and humorous way."

If you and your children enjoy sophisticated, irreverent humor very much in the tradition of Shel Silverstein, inspired by the wonderful Danny Kaye recordings of the fifties, treat yourselves to at least one Barry Louis Polisar recording. It would be nearly negligent to deprive yourselves of the chance to experience his magic.

Barry's songs are being recorded by many other performers, including Peter Alsop, Mary Miché, and Charlotte Diamond. But for performances with extra-special insight, Barry's original recordings are unique.

Additional titles by Barry Louis Polisar include *Naughty Songs for Boys and Girls, Songs for Well-Behaved Children, Stanley Stole My Shoelace and Rubbed It in His Armpit and Other Songs My Parents Won't Let Me Sing,* and his newest release, *Juggling Babies and a Career.*

I Eat Kids and Other Songs for Rebellious Children (1975)
Rainbow Morning Music
2121 Fairland Road
Silver Spring, MD 20904
Format: Cassette, LP
Age Appeal: 5–9
Material: Outrageous, often realistic songs about childhood
Vocals: Barry Louis Polisar
Vocal Style: Folk
Instrumentation: Guitar

While many of the songs on this album are given a more animated performance on *Captured Live and in the Act,* this album also contains outrageous Polisar gems available only here.

Highlights include "I Don't Brush My Teeth and I Never Comb My Hair," which talks about the consequences of being smelly and dirty; "My Dentist Is an Awfully Nice Man," a fantasy about the perfect dentist, who fills kids' teeth with candy; "I Eat Kids," Barry's answer to how vegetarians get enough protein; "I Never Did Like You, Anyhow," a wish list of how a rebellious child might confront the arbitrary rules of life; and "I Don't Believe You're Going to the Bathroom," which portrays a hostile teacher who gets what all kids will think she or he deserves.

"I Sneaked into the Kitchen in the Middle of the Night," a personal favorite of mine, is a first-person narrative about how a kid uses his baby brother to take the blame for eating all the chocolate cake.

My Brother Thinks He's a Banana
and Other Provocative Songs for Children (1977)

Rainbow Morning Music
Format: Cassette, LP
Age Appeal: 5–9
Material: Songs about family issues and school conflicts
Vocals: Barry Louis Polisar
Vocal Style: Folk
Instrumentation: Guitar, harmonica, snickers, snores, barks, croaks, and giggles

On this album Barry has created songs that deal with the contemporary reordering of roles as we have known them. He also continues to poke fun at traditional family and school conflicts with irreverent humor. Children and adults will find much to discuss. Included in this collection are two Polisar masterpieces. "My Brother Threw Up on My Stuffed Toy Bunny" may cause fainthearted adults to shudder, but will benefit every kid who hears Barry combine humor, pathos, realism, and philosophy. "My Mommy Drives a Dump Truck" speaks about role reversals as Barry defends people's rights to make nontraditional choices.

Additional songs of note are "The Skatter-Brak-Flath Who Lives in My Bath," which depicts a cooperative creature who is the reason Barry can't get clean; "My Brother Thinks He's a Banana," Barry's ode to weird siblings (adults will have to explain many of the sophisticated images to young listeners, but that's fine); "Our Dog Bernard," a Polisar classic that has been recorded by several other artists, telling the tale of a dog who makes surprising choices in his life; "For My Sister, Wherever I May Find Her," describing how Barry unexpectedly transforms his nasty sister into an apple tree covered with sour apples; "But I'm Just Thirteen," which uses graphic images to paint the classic efforts of a maturing child to deny responsibilities; and "Talking I Got a Teacher and He's So Boring," a call-it-like-you-see-it description of a teacher who lacks effective teaching techniques and classroom sensitivity.

Barry Louis Polisar Captured Live and in the Act (1978)
Rainbow Morning Music
Format: Cassette, LP
Age Appeal: 5–9
Material: Outrageous, on-target songs about childhood
Vocals: Barry Louis Polisar
Vocal Style: Folk
Instrumentation: Guitar

The special zaniness of Barry Louis Polisar is never more evident than on this live-performance recording. Barry's articulate introductions and colorful performances coupled with the unabashed laughter and audience participation go a long way toward illustrating his appeal to elementary-age audiences. A collection of songs from three earlier Polisar recordings, this sampler may be the best choice for a first taste of his irreverent world.

The highlight of this recording is the infamous "I Got a Teacher, She's So Mean," in which Barry paints an exaggerated picture of a monstrous human being that may offend adults, especially educators. It would be the best of all worlds if children always loved their teachers; but, sad to say, they do not. Sometimes children do not understand what is expected of them; sometimes teachers create adversarial situations in their classrooms. An enduring hit on radio's Kids America, "I Got a Teacher, She's So Mean" excites and satisfies kids who need a vehicle for complaining about a part of their lives in which they are traditionally powerless.

Additional songs include "Early Sunday Morning," every mischievous child's fantasy of the perfect food fight, complete with a discussion of the consequences of being caught; "He Eats Asparagus, Why Can't You Be That Way," depicting the perfect boy next door whom parents forever hold up as a model for their own "imperfect" children; "I'm a Three-Toed, Triple-Eyed, Double-Jointed Dinosaur," about a rough-and-tumble yet irresistible monster; "My Friend Jake," portraying a nonconformist who finds the world more palatable by dealing with it upside down; "Thump, Thump, Thump," which describes the fear and tension created by the unknown; "Tomorrow," a dialogue about procrastination between a parent and a child who finds it's convenient to put off doing everything but eating chocolate cake; "Fred," the story of a horrible, mean monster whom no one takes seriously because of his unmonsterlike name; "When the House Is Dark and Quiet," which tells the tale of two children who pride themselves on confounding baby-sitters (while Barry describes behavior too dangerous and cruel—I would hope—to emulate, the children in the audience are vicariously thrilled by his audacity); "The Apple of My Eye," about falling in love with a cyclops, which tells listeners that when you love someone, you realize that it doesn't matter what he looks like; "Shut Up in the Library," portraying an insensitive, cartoonlike librarian (once again, Barry's overblown portrait sends a reassuring message to kids that he too has had to cope with irrational adults); "Don't Put Your Finger Up Your Nose," an irresistible sing-along that children adore for its outrageousness; and "Louder," a scream-along song in which kids learn that following directions can be fun.

Off-Color Songs for Kids (1983)

Rainbow Morning Music
Format: Cassette, LP
Age Appeal: 5–9
Material: Outspoken, humorous songs and poems which promote positive values and decry intolerance
Vocals: Barry Louis Polisar
Vocal Style: Folk
Instrumentation: Guitars, accordion, percussion

The songs on this album stress the importance of individuality and feeling good about oneself; some warn against being judgmental and intolerant of others. On the home front, Barry continues to acknowledge the eternal sibling war and the everpresent need for patience.

"Underwear," with its Bo Diddley beat, is a Polisar masterpiece. Kids love its risqué lyrics, and in between the laughs there's a great message: we are all equal underneath.

"Town of Round" is a parable about what happens to people who can't tolerate having among them someone of a different shape.

"I'd Be Me" is a properson song. After telling us why he would not want to be a movie star or president, Barry shares his important philosophy in a singable chorus: "Like yourself a lot."

"I Forgot," delivered with a realistic and humorous whine, lists all the things a kid has forgotten, including taking out the garbage, finding his way to school, and cleaning his room since last December.

"I Looked into the Mirror, What Did the Mirror Say?" is another raucous Polisar creation, which will have the kids roaring while they hear that who they are is important, not how they look.

"Caterpillar" is the saga of an insect who longs for the glamour and excitement of being a butterfly. But once she attains her goal, her glory is short-lived: she ends up getting caught in a butterfly net.

"The Crab," a short poem, is a delicious portrait of a grumpy crustacean—or is it a person we all know?

Kids can really appreciate "Oh No! I Like My Sister." When she's away, Barry misses her; but when she comes back, nothing has changed.

With its humorous historic references, "Water" is a song that focuses on the history and importance of this essential element.

"Elvin and the Witch: A Song About Politics and Friendship" is a cautionary tale about discrimination. Children laugh at Elvin, shun him, and hurt his feelings. But he becomes good friends with the witch on the hill. As a result, when the kids go to the woods to hide from Elvin, the witch grabs them and eats them. Barry sums up his story with a sophisticated message.

"What If a Zebra Had Spots" is a song that asks us if we would like the world better if animals and people were rearranged.

The last two songs on *Off-Color Songs for Kids* are a matched pair. "Five More Minutes" describes how adults can be the world's worst procrastinators when it comes to spending time with their kids. "Later" describes how this familiar delay tactic is overused and abused by parents.

Raffi

Raffi is the first genuine superstar of family music. At this writing he has released nine albums, which have collectively sold more than six million recordings. He has published a host of songbooks, picture books, and videos, has won numerous awards for excellence, and has been given major coverage in *The New York Times, The Washington Post, The Wall Street Journal, The Christian Science Monitor* and *People* magazine as well as many other newspapers and parenting magazines. In 1987–88 he toured seventy cities, giving more than one hundred fifty performances to sold-out audiences. He also gives keynote addresses at educational conferences.

Who is this modern-day Pied Piper? He is a gentle, eloquent man with a genuine gift for unifying families through shared music listening. Accentuating the positive,

Raffi collects, writes, and sings songs that celebrate life and family with dignity and warmth.

Born in Egypt of Armenian parents in 1948, Raffi Cavoukian immigrated to Canada when he was ten. In 1974, when he was attempting to establish himself as a folk singer for adults, his mother-in-law, Daphne Pike, invited him to perform for her nursery school class. Raffi admits readily that at that point he knew nothing about North American children's songs. His wife, Debi Pike, a longtime kindergarten teacher, taught him the words to "Baa Baa Black Sheep" and "Eentsy Weentsy Spider."

Sitting on the nursery school floor with his guitar, surrounded by singing, clapping, and dancing three-to-five-year-olds, Raffi made a startling discovery. Not only did the kids love what he was doing—*he* was having a good time too. Soon Raffi was performing in schools all over Toronto.

By 1976, again encouraged by Daphne Pike, Raffi made his first recording, *Singable Songs for the Very Young.* In Toronto it became an instant success. "People were buying it in fours and fives to give to their friends, saying they'd never heard anything like it," reports Raffi in an interview in the *Christian Science Monitor.* "The record's immediate popularity caused quite an identity crisis. What kind of performer was I?"

Intending to maintain his career as an adult performer, Raffi finally had to face the fact that his audiences at children's concerts were growing by leaps and bounds while the audiences for his adult performances were stagnating. Eventually Raffi made peace with himself and dug into the world of music for children. "I realized not only that I needn't be ashamed of giving up adult folk singing, but that something rare was happening here. Not everyone can entertain children. . . . Many popular stars of the day will tell you they'd be terrified to entertain children."

While young children need no convincing, it seems that most of the adult world still needs a lot of educating about the importance and value of Raffi's gentle gifts. "Sometimes people say to me, 'Let's talk about your work for children first, and then we can talk about your serious work,'" Raffi has said. "That kind of answer comes from not understanding that children are whole people, like you and me. Children *are* my serious work, and that means respecting them as an audience, the way I would respect any adult audience."

Raffi's commitment to his young audience has grown and intensified since those early days of singing in nursery schools. With Debi's help, Raffi has developed a strong philosophy about children. "I read everything I can get my hands on," he says. "I try to promote a vision of children as whole people, not lesser because they are smaller, but people whose perceptions are unique. There's absolutely no need to be condescending to a child if you feel the way I do. I value them the way they are. I'm not hurrying them, not pushing them to grow up before their time."

In addition to creating a unique blend of music dedicated to the dignity of childhood, Raffi did something that changed the way adults thought about "kids' music": he marketed his recordings where they would catch the eye of today's new breed of concerned parent. Upscale toy shops, bookstores, and even trendy children's clothing shops began to carry a complete line of Raffi records and tapes. Back in 1983, that was *all* the music they carried.

The time was right, the sound was right; and Raffi was able to establish a vast audience for himself the way no performer for family audiences had ever done before. And in creating his own success, Raffi fathered an important grass-roots music movement in Canada and the United States. Parents who enjoyed Raffi recordings with their very young children became eager for more and different family listening.

Many other talented songwriters and performers, seeing Raffi make his mark, began to reach out to family audiences with their own innovative additions to the growing body of contemporary music. Following the pathways pioneered by Raffi, many independent artists are able to make their musical presence known in homes, schools, and day care facilities across the country. Thank you, Raffi!

In addition to the recordings described below, titles include *More Singable Songs* (1977), *Rise and Shine* (1982), *Raffi's Christmas Album* (1983), *One Light, One Sun* (1985), and *Everything Grows* (1987).

Singable Songs for the Very Young (1976)

Troubadour Records Ltd.
1075 Cambie St.
Vancouver, B.C., Canada V6B 5L7
Distributed in the U.S. by MCA
70 Universal City Plaza
Universal City, CA 91608
Format: Cassette, LP
Age Appeal: All ages
Target Ages: 2–5

Material: Traditional and original material gently celebrating life
Vocals: Raffi with Ken Whitely
Vocal Style: Warm, velvety folk voice
Instrumentation: Guitars, mandolin, banjo, harmonica, accordion, piano, percussion, trumpet, flute, electric piano, spoons, jug, washboard, bells, Dobro, fiddle, jaw harp, kazoo

Here's a warm and gentle, now classic recording that belongs in every home. Songs include "The More We Get Together," "Down by the Bay," "Brush Your Teeth," "Robin in the Rain," "Five Little Frogs," "I Wonder If I'm Growing," "Aiken Drum," "Bumping Up and Down," "Must Be Santa," "Willoughby, Wallaby, Woo," "The Spider on the Floor," "Baa Baa Black Sheep," "Going to the Zoo," "My Dreydel," "Peanut Butter Sandwich," "Five Little Pumpkins," "The Sharing Song," "Mr. Sun," and "Old MacDonald Had a Band."

The Corner Grocery Store (1979)
Troubador Records Ltd.
Age Appeal: 3–5
(See *Singable Songs for the Very Young* above for details.)

Another gentle treat from Raffi, songs include "You'll Sing a Song and I'll Sing a Song," "Pick a Bale o' Cotton," "Frère Jacques," "There Came a Girl from France," "Cluck, Cluck, Red Hen," "Boom, Boom," "My Way Home," "Les Zombis et Les Loups-Garous," "Swing Low, Sweet Chariot," "Anansi," "The Corner Grocery Store," "Jig Along Home," "Popcorn," "Y a un rat," "Sur le pont d'Avignon," "Going on a Picnic," "Rock-A-Bye, Baby," and "Good Night, Irene."

Baby Beluga (1980)
Troubador Records Ltd.
Age Appeal: All ages
Target Ages: 3–6
(See *Singable Songs for the Very Young* above for details.)

A major winner and my personal favorite, *Baby Beluga* makes a great baby or birthday gift. Songs include the Raffi masterpieces "Baby Beluga" and "All I Really Need" as well as "Biscuits in the Oven," "Oats and Beans and Barley," "Day-O," "Thanks a Lot," "To Everyone in All the World," "Over in the Meadow," "This Old Man," "Water Dance," "Kumbaya," "Joshua Giraffe," and "Morningtown Ride."

Sally Rogers

While Sally Rogers has been actively recording and touring for several years, sharing songs of humanity and peace, just recently she has begun to use her warm, expressive folk voice and magical way with the guitar and dulcimer to sing songs oriented to childhood.

Sally produces her own biannual newsletter in which she lists her upcoming performance schedule and writes thoughtfully about music, life, and human rights. For more information, write to Sally Rogers, P.O. Box 111, Pomfret, Connecticut 06250.

Peace by Peace (1988)

Golden Music
Western Publishing
1220 Mound Ave.
Racine, WI 53404
Format: Cassette
Age Appeal: 5–9
Material: Songs of empowerment, self-determination, and peace, written by Sally Rogers, Malvina Reynolds, Bob Blue, Cathy Fink, and others.
Vocals: Sally Rogers with children's chorus
Vocal Style: Melodious folk
Instrumentation: guitar, mountain dulcimer, piano, synthesizer, mandolin, banjo, fiddle

Sally Rogers has written and collected positive, poetic songs which promote the principles of being kind, just, and responsible. Singing primarily from a child's point of view, she performs with an affecting combination of reality and humor—and a remarkable absence of condescension. If you believe that global peace starts at home, this is an album that you will want to share with your family.

The issues of peace may seem heavy, but Sally balances them so easily that they give the illusion of being light. Teachers, day care workers, and librarians will find the songs on *Peace by Peace* infectiously singable and sensitive, ideal for sharing with their children.

Highlights include "I've Got a Song," celebrating the promise of life to come and the potential of all children; "I Wanna Be Somebody (Who Somebody Like Me Could Like)," with an engaging chantlike quality that makes it a great song for family car rides and school performances; "Magic Penny," with lovely harmonies by a chorus of children; "I Can Be Anything I Want to Be," about self-determination and the ultimate truth that what we do best is be ourselves; "The Lambeth Children," which recounts the true story of fifty children who successfully saved eleven maple trees from being cut down; and "Hands," which describes the different ways cooperative hands enhance everyone's life. "Dear Mr. President" tells the tale of two children who, competing for the biggest sticker collection, end up punching each other. While it may leave your five-to-nine-year-old laughing, it is a peace song that deserves a lot of family and classroom discussion.

ROSENSHONTZ

Gary Rosen and Bill Shontz began working together in 1974. Describing themselves as "part Simon and Garfunkel, part Smothers Brothers," they played everywhere—from Irish bars to Mexican restaurants. But they got the best responses to their music when they played outside Manhattan's Central Park Zoo. "Kids really liked what we did," explained Gary Rosen in an interview in *The Boston Globe,* "and they made their parents stop and then put money in the hat." Writing more songs for kids, they performed at birthday parties for five-year-olds on the Upper East Side.

ROSENSHONTZ released its first album for children in 1980. Emphasizing audience participation, the duo established a more than full-time touring schedule which had them giving back-to-back family performances in schools, universities, museums, performing-arts centers, and concert halls across the United States and Canada. ROSENSHONTZ has appeared on the "Today" show, on the Disney Channel, and on radio's "Morning Edition," "Woody's Children," and "Kids America."

By fusing classic rock 'n' roll rhythms with upbeat, family-centered lyrics, RO-SENSHONTZ has helped pioneer the movement for quality family entertainment in the United States. With five award-winning recordings and a video at this writing, it has created a sound and sensibility that spans the generations. "I think a big reason for our success," explains Bill Shontz, "is that we write for adults as well as kids in the same song—the best material works on more than one level."

Choose ROSENSHONTZ recordings according to the age-appeal ratings below. If you have a three-to-five-year-old, don't miss *Tickles You!* and *Share It. Rock 'n' Roll Teddy Bear, It's the Truth,* and *Family Vacation* are for elementary-age listeners.

Tickles You! (1980)

RS Records

P.O. Box 651

Brattleboro, VT 05301

Format: Cassette, LP

Age Appeal: 3–6

Material: Humorous songs with imaginative images; most songs written by Gary Rosen and Bill Shontz; lyrics included

Vocals: Gary Rosen and Bill Shontz

Vocal Style: Clean, soaring harmonies in folk-rock style

Instrumentation: Acoustic and electric guitars, flutes, clarinets, pennywhistle, saxophone, drum kit, congas, quica, temple blocks, sandpaper, shakers, bass kalimba, quiro, tambourine, wind chimes, cowbell, nose horn

Back in 1980 *The New York Times* called *Tickles You!* "clever . . . beautiful . . . poetic . . . and inventive." This inspired recording has become a classic, containing such gems as "Sam the Tickle Man," "Life Is," "Imagination," "I Wish I Was," "Noses," "These Are the Questions," and "Hippopotamus Rock." If you are just getting started listening to music with your preschooler, this album is a must-have!

Share It (1982)

RS Records

Format: Cassette, LP

Age Appeal: 3–6

Material: Contemporary, sophisticated, witty songs about childhood experiences and sensibilities; most material by Gary Rosen and Bill Shontz; lyrices included

Vocals: Gary Rosen, Bill Shontz, and children's chorus

Vocal Style: Exuberant folk-rock

Instrumentation: Guitars, mandolin, mandocello, flute, saxophones, clarinet, recorders, trumpet, trombone, flugelhorn, percussion, timbales

A great follow-up to *Tickles You!,* this recording includes such treasures as "Share It"; "Pet Sounds," which borrows delightfully from the Beach Boys; "Sleep, Sleep," which my eleven-year-old and I still sing to each other; and the touching "Mandolin Song."

It's the Truth (1984)

RS Records

Format: Cassette, LP

Age Appeal: 5–8

Material: Songs about homework, messy rooms, sugar consumption, teasing, and friendship handled with humor and sensitivity; most material by Rosen and Shontz with Storey; lyrics included

Vocals: Gary Rosen and Bill Shontz

Vocal style: Exuberant folk-rock

Instrumentation: Guitars, flute, saxophones, clarinet, pennywhistle, trumpet, trombone, percussion

Addressing a slightly older audience, this classic album contains the very funny "Don't Bring It Home," a mother's plea to her child; "It's the Truth," in which Rosen and Shontz offer fanciful reasons why their homework isn't done and their room is a mess; "Sugar," which addresses our intergenerational craving for sweets; and "Hugga Hugga," an exuberant song that will make listeners want to hug each other—as well as Gary and Bill.

Rock 'n' Roll Teddy Bear (1986)

RS Records

Format: Cassette, LP

Age Appeal: 4–6

Material: Contemporary, witty songs, mostly by Rosen/Shontz/Storey; lyrics included

Vocals: Gary Rosen and Bill Shontz with backup vocals

Vocal Style: Exuberant rock 'n' roll

Instrumentation: Guitars, flute, saxophones, clarinet, piano, synthesizer, emulator, percussion

With a strong rock-pop sound, this fanciful recording focuses on friendship and determination. Highlights include "ROSENSHONTZ Rap," "Go for It," "Rock 'n' Roll Teddy Bear," "Little Light of Mine," and "The Best That I Can."

Family Vacation (1988)

RS Records

Format: Cassette, LP

Age Appeal: 5–8

Material: Contemporary, witty, touching songs, mostly by Rosen/Shontz/Storey; lyrics included

Vocals: Gary Rosen and Bill Shontz with backup vocals, including children's chorus

Vocal Style: Exuberant, harmonic rock 'n' roll

Instrumentation: Acoustic and electric guitars, flutes, saxophones, trumpet, clarinet, keyboards, synthesizer, emulator, percussion

Family Vacation contains songs with sounds inspired by the sixties and the eighties and lyrics that are contemporary, humorous, and touching. Highlights include "Family Vacation," which describes the struggles of leaving the house together to start a trip; "Dear Diary," a moving confession about the worries of becoming part of a blended family; "Daddy Does the Dishes," a prizewinning ode to Sam Cooke and "Chain Gang"; and "Better Say No," which imaginatively describes how to avoid potentially threatening situations.

Phil Rosenthal

For recordings that deliver traditional American folk favorites with the flavor, texture, and elegance they deserve, turn your attention to the work of Phil Rosenthal and his company, American Melody. A nine-year veteran of a well-respected adult-oriented bluegrass band, in 1986 Phil decided to refocus his energy on music for family listening. He has, at this writing, produced five splendid albums, on two of which he is the star performer.

"In a way, I hate to call them children's albums or children's music," Phil has said. "It's mostly folk songs that have been handed down through the ages." Phil is right. While the tunes on his recordings may be those we associate with childhood, they are performed and produced with a dignity and skill that set them up to be satisfying listening for people of all generations. In addition, Phil Rosenthal as producer has established a signature sound of gentle but spirited vocals and crystalline mandolin, banjo, guitar, and fiddle music, which comes through clear and strong on even the flimsiest plastic child-oriented tape player.

Turkey in the Straw (1985)

American Melody Records
P.O. Box 270
Guilford, CT 06347
Format: Cassette
Age Appeal: All ages
Target Ages: 2–5
Material: Traditional and updated folk music
Vocals: Phil Rosenthal, with backup by Ann Vaughn and vocals by Naomi Rosenthal, age nine
Vocal Style: Bluegrass, with gentle and upbeat harmonies
Instrumentation: Banjo, mandolin, guitar

Turkey in the Straw includes the traditional "It Ain't Gonna Rain No More," "Bingo," "Twinkle, Twinkle, Little Star," "Aiken Drum," "Little Liza Jane," and "Turkey in the Straw" as well as "Open Up the Window, Noah" with updated lyrics and two original compositions by Phil Rosenthal, "The Snowy Day" and "Listen to the Bluegrass."

Paw Paw Patch (1987)

American Melody Records
Format: Cassette
Age Appeal: All ages
Target Ages: 2–5
Material: Traditional folk music in the bluegrass style

Paw Paw Patch contains more traditional American folk tunes skillfully performed by Phil Rosenthal and company. Included are "Paw Paw Patch," "Mary Had a Little Lamb," "Looby Loo," "Polly Wolly Doodle," "I'm a Little Tea Pot," and "Skip to My Lou" as well as Oscar Brand's contemporary classic "When I First Came to This Land."

Grandma's Patchwork Quilt (1987)

American Melody Records
Format: Cassette
Age Appeal: 3–8
Material: Traditional and original folk music

Vocals: Cathy Fink, Jonathan Edwards, Larry Penn, Naomi Rosenthal, Phil Rosenthal, and John McCutcheon
Vocal Style: Folk
Instrumentation: Banjo, guitar, mandolin

Produced by Phil Rosenthal, *Grandma's Patchwork Quilt* is a collection of songs performed by a remarkable group of performers. Highlights include Cathy Fink delivering toe-tapping versions of "Zip-A-Dee-Doo-Dah" and "Buffalo Gals" to her own virtuosic banjo accompaniment; Jonathan Edwards singing "Three Blind Mice" as a wonderfully silly saga, written by John W. Ivimey, of what *really* happened to the three blind mice (finally someone has made sense of a long-incomprehensible Mother Goose rhyme—this is a song *everyone* should hear); Larry Penn giving an affecting, gravelly-voiced performance of his "I'm a Little Cookie," a simple yet moving song which supports the value of all things and people in all conditions; "A Duck Named Earl," with lyrics written by Beth Sommers Rosenthal, a humorous, bluegrass-style song sung by Phil Rosenthal, who accompanies himself with energetic mandolin and guitar picking; and John McCutcheon's "Awful Hilly Daddy Willy Trip," with humorous yet touching lyrics about an endless car ride through the back roads of North Carolina.

Kevin Roth

Virtuoso mountain dulcimer player Kevin Roth, who has performed on more than fifteen recordings for adults, has created several award-winning recordings for family listening. Velvet-voiced Kevin sings primarily traditional songs as he accompanies himself on the gossamer-sounding dulcimer, backed up by a host of other instruments. Commenting on his distinctive and calming sound, *American Baby* magazine has said, "Roth's music is as sweet and rich as a cup of cocoa."

Kevin's mellow music must be paired with the right listeners at the right time of day. Parents and young children may find his smooth voice just what they need to unwind together. A child who has trouble falling asleep may be comforted and encouraged by Kevin's rich, peaceful, reassuring lullaby album, while a rambunctious child on the move may not want to stop long enough to focus on the mellow yet activity-oriented sound of other Roth albums. For a restless child confined in the car, however, a Kevin Roth recording may be just the tool to soften the atmosphere—provided Kevin doesn't relax the driver to the point where he or she wants to doze off too!

Also by Kevin Roth on CMS: the award-winning *Animal Crackers*.

Lullabies for Little Dreamers (1985)

CMS Records
226 Washington St.
Mount Vernon, NY 10553
Format: Cassette, LP
Age Appeal: 1–3
Material: Traditional and contemporary lullabies
Vocals: Kevin Roth
Vocal Style: Tuneful, tranquil, and mellow
Instrumentation: Mountain dulcimer, keyboard

Highlights of this album, with its velvety, restful sound, include "All Through the Night," "Hush, Little Baby," "Are You Sleeping/Twinkle, Twinkle," "When You Wish Upon a Star," "Over the Rainbow," Brahms's "Lullaby," "Roll Over," and "Skye Boat Song."

Oscar, Bingo and Buddies (1986)

CMS Records
Format: Cassette, LP
Age Appeal: 2–5
Material: Traditional folk and camp songs and original songs
Vocals: Kevin Roth
Vocal Style: Mellow and tuneful
Instrumentation: Mountain dulcimer, keyboard

Highlights include "Oscar," "Do Your Ears Hang Low/Giggles/Old MacDonald Had a Farm," "Animal Fair," "You Make me So Happy/You Are My Sunshine," "Bingo," "The Bear Went over the Mountain/On Top of Old Smokey/This Old Man," "I've Been Working on the Railroad/She'll be Comin' Round the Mountain," "The Green Grass Grows All Around," and "He's Got the Whole World in His Hands."

Unbearable Bears (1986)

Marlboro Records

845 Marlboro Spring Rd.

Kennet Square, PA 19348

Format: Cassette, LP

Age Appeal: 2–5

Material: Songs mostly about bears, some familiar, others written for this album by Kevin Roth

Vocals: Kevin Roth

Vocal Style: mellow, upbeat, and tuneful

Instrumentation: Mountain dulcimer, keyboards, flute, guitar, drums, percussion, oboe, English horn, tuba, saxophone, clarinet

Families and classroom groups where bears are a central interest will find *Unbearable Bears* irresistible. In addition to a large helping of songs that focus on bear fantasies, notable highlights include Kevin's gentle interpretation of the Elvis Presley classic "(Let Me Be Your) Teddy Bear"; "The Garden," written by Roth after the Frog and Toad stories by Arnold Lobel; and "You Are You," which celebrates individuality and the need of people to know that others care about them.

Additional titles: "That Bear Makes Me Crazy," "Teddy Bears' Picnic," "Honey Bear," "The Show Biz Bear," "The Unbearable Bears," "The Bear You Loved," "That Bear Snores," and "Lullaby Bears."

Pete Seeger

An inspired and passionate singer, storyteller, banjo picker, songwriter, music publisher, human rights and environmental crusader, Pete Seeger has been the most influential folk performer of our time, a leading force behind the flourishing of American folk music as we know it today. Pete's continued energy through the darkest of times has inspired people to sing out about the events, feelings, and values that affect humanity. Thanks to Pete Seeger, "music with a message" has become an effective way for people to communicate and share and grow.

In his book *How Can I Keep From Singing: Pete Seeger,* David King Dunaway has said, "If anyone in the United States has inspired people to make their own music, it has been Pete Seeger. He was, it will be remembered, a great believer in the magical powers of song."

Pete began his recording career in 1941 and has since performed on more than one hundred albums, singing songs that reflect America's musical heritage and define its musical future. In the early sixties Pete recorded a number of albums showcasing what he considered to be the best new songs printed in *Broadside* magazine. On the back of the album Pete addressed a question that we continue to ask today: how can contemporary compositions be folk songs?

"Face it," Seeger said, "there are several different definitions of folk music, and these songs might fit one definition, but would certainly not fit another. For myself, I don't think it matters all that much. The important thing is: are they good songs? Do they sing well? Is the poetry so good you can't get it out of your head? Are the words true, and do they need saying? Does the music move you?" Pointing out that there are certain obvious differences between what is usually considered a "folk" song and the usual "pop" song, Pete defines the former as a song that is "often concerned with controversial subjects. They may be short or long, or ignore the Big Beat, and other juke box requirements."

Pete has been America's most outspoken and influential troubadour for more than fifty years, yet not many people know that both his parents were classically trained musicians. And not just Pete but three more of the seven Seeger children became leaders in the growth of American folk music.

Despite his disinterest in classical training, Pete Seeger was dramatically influenced by his father, Charles, and his stepmother, Ruth Crawford Seeger, both dedicated and politically aware musicologists. While he shunned formal piano and voice lessons, at age eight Pete was playing the ukulele; at age thirteen, the four-string banjo; and at nineteen, the five-string banjo.

In 1935, at the age of sixteen, Pete traveled to the folk festival at Asheville, North Carolina, where he heard banjo and guitar music that profoundly shaped his life. He attended Harvard briefly but left in the late 1930s to travel across America with his banjo. Listening to hundreds of folk musicians sing and play, he assimilated their tunes and styles, developing his own magical musical persona.

With his zesty, bell-like voice, magnificent musicianship, and intense feeling for the power of songs and of people, Pete Seeger is an American treasure. Although he has recorded more than ten albums of songs specifically for young listeners, to my mind many more of Pete's recordings make great family listening. Especially appropriate are the joyful, dynamic recordings he made in the 1950s and '60s as part of the dynamic group the Weavers as well as those he recorded with Arlo Guthrie.

American Folksongs for Children (1954)
Smithsonian / Folkways Records
Smithsonian Institution
Office of Folklife Programs
955 L'Enfant Plaza, Suite 2600
Washington, D.C. 20560
Distributed by Rounder Records
1 Camp St.
Cambridge, MA 02140
Format: Cassette, LP
Age Appeal: All ages
Target Ages: 2–5
Material: Traditional tunes; song sheet included
Vocals: Pete Seeger
Vocal Style: Zesty folk
Instrumentation: Five-string banjo

In Pete Seeger's historic collections of folk songs for very young children you will discover that a few of the lyrics are outdated by our contemporary "consciousness." Rather than shy away from these masterpieces of music, rhythm, and poetry, treat the offending lyrics (and there really aren't many) with the same direct family discussions about human values as you would (one hopes) treat any other objectionable attitude that you and your family view on television, in the movies, or hear in Top 40 songs. There are more objectionable messages out there in the wide world of broadcasting than on any album of traditional music for kids. Yet, sad to say, it is the rare parent who sits and discusses with children the offensive behavior and attitudes exhibited on television sitcoms. Nor do many parents prevent their families from watching.

   Highlights include "Bought Me a Cat," "Jim Crack Corn," "Train Is a-Coming," "Frog Went a-Courting," "Clap Your Hands," and "She'll Be Coming Round the Mountain."

Birds, Beasts, Bugs and Little Fishes (1955)
Birds, Beasts, Bugs and Bigger Fishes (1955)
Abiyoyo (and Other Story Songs for Children) (1967)
Smithsonian / Folkways Records
Distributed by Rounder Records

Format: Cassette, LP
Age Appeal: All ages
Target Ages: 2–5
Material: Traditional tunes inspired by and dedicated to the songbooks of Ruth
Crawford Seeger
Vocals: Pete Seeger
Vocal Style: Zesty folk
Instrumentation: Five-string banjo

Selections in *Little Fishes* include "Fly Through My Window," "I Had a Rooster,"
"Frog Went a-Courtin'," "I Know an Old Lady (Who Swallowed a Fly)," "Teency
Weency Spider," and "My Little Kitty." Highlights from *Bigger Fishes* include "Leath-
erwing Bat," "Mole in the Ground," "The Fox," "Old Paint," "The Elephant," and
"The Foolish Frog."

"Abiyoyo" is the quintessential musical story, which Pete Seeger magically weaves
around a simple tune. Ostracized because they are such nuisances and practical
jokers, a ukulele-playing boy and his magician father manage to save their town
from destruction by a terrible giant. Based on a Bantu legend from South Africa,
it's a spunky, bittersweet, and optimistic tale to be savored by all families.

Pete Seeger and Brother Kirk Visit Sesame Street (1974)

Children's Records of America
159 W. 53rd St.
New York, NY 10019
Format: LP
Target Ages: 3–6
Material: Traditional and new songs that encourage singing along
Vocals: Pete Seeger, Brother Kirkpatrick, and "Sesame Street" cast members
Vocal Style: Folk
Instrumentation: Banjo, guitar

With Big Bird and Oscar the Grouch singing and talking with Pete Seeger and
Brother Kirk, this is a gem of a recording for fans of "Sesame Street." In addition
to the traditional tunes, it contains timely "new" songs Pete included back in 1974
which have since developed into contemporary classics of family listening.

The album was hard to find even when it was in print, but with all the current
activity in the field of family listening, perhaps someone will think to reissue this

one. Meantime, look for *Pete Seeger and Brother Kirk Visit Sesame Street* at garage sales, flea markets, and out-of-print-record shops. It has a bright green cover.

Highlights include "Michael Row the Boat Ashore," "This Land is Your Land," "She'll Be Coming Round the Mountain," "Patty Cake the Gorilla," "Garbage," "The Ballad of Martin Luther King," and "Guantanamera."

Circles and Seasons (1979)

Warner Bros. Records
3300 Warner Blvd.
Burbank, CA 91505
Format: Cassette, LP
Age Appeal: All ages
Material: Contemporary and traditional songs; lyrics included
Vocals: Pete Seeger with backup vocals by Fred Hellerman, Ronnie Gilbert
Vocal Style: Contemporary folk
Instrumentation: Twelve-string guitar, banjo, bongos, bass, xylophone, drums, glock, keyboard, percussion, recorder, brass

Out of print but worth searching for, *Circles and Seasons* brought Pete Seeger together with former Weaver Fred Hellerman as producer and arranger. It's a dynamic collaboration that offers timely contemporary songs produced with compelling, well-developed sound. While the album was intended for adult listeners, it has a clarity of vision and a musical exuberance that make it perfect for family listening.

Several of the titles, you may notice, have become standards on recordings for children; others deserve to be. Highlights include "Garbage," "Sailing Down This Golden River," "I'm Gonna Be an Engineer," "Seneca Canoe Song," "Maple Syrup Time," "Garden Song," "Allelulia/Joy Upon This Earth."

Pete Seeger and Arlo Guthrie Together in Concert (1975)

Warner Bros. Records
Format: Cassette, LP
Age Appeal: All ages
Material: Contemporary and traditional songs
Vocals: Pete Seeger and Arlo Guthrie
Vocal Style: Contemporary folk
Instrumentation: Guitars, banjo, keyboard

Here's a great family-listening album, a two-record set that may be hard to find. Highlights include "Way Out There," "Yodeling," "Declaration of Independence," "Get Up and Go," "May There Always Be Sunshine," "Three Rules of Discipline and Eight Rules of Attention," "Stealin'," and "Guantanamera."

Sharon, Lois and Bram

With combined record sales nearing two million copies, a list of prestigious awards (including one for their "Elephant Show" on the Nickelodeon network, which reaches an estimated 43 million households daily), a host of videos, and a hectic international touring schedule, Sharon, Lois and Bram have become a genuine phenomenon. Musically rich and diverse, and seemingly tireless, they're often called the Peter, Paul and Mary of children's music.

Canadian-based Sharon Hampson, Lois Lilienstein, and Bram Morrison put in many years as individual performers for adult audiences, but it was their interest in educating children that eventually drew them together. In 1978, as participants of Mariposa in the Schools, an innovative Canadian program that brings folk music to children, Sharon, Lois and Bram decided to pool their resources and repertoires and make a record together. Borrowing $20,000 from family and friends, they cut their first album, *One Elephant, Deux Elephants*.

Sharon, Lois and Bram have gone on to make (at this writing) nine albums, each a colorful potpourri of songs—old family favorites, childhood classics, and traditional folk songs from around the world as well as jazz, swing, music-hall, and rock 'n' roll standards. With their strong, energetic vocal style, and high-powered musicians such as Bill Usher and Eric Nagler to back them up, their recordings offer a full, fun, fast-paced sound perfect for family listening.

With such a lengthy list of children's recordings, where does the first-time listener start? At the beginning, naturally. While you'll hardly go wrong with any Sharon, Lois and Bram recording, their earliest recordings radiate a freshness that's hard to match. Of course, *Mainly Mother Goose* is especially appropriate for very young listeners.

While the music of Sharon, Lois and Bram does not deal with specific issues, it offers families rich, enjoyable listening experiences that will go a long way toward helping children grow into diverse, worldly listeners. Each Sharon, Lois and Bram recording contains such a generous selection of songs that the listings below represent merely an overview. All recordings come with illustrated song guides.

In addition to the titles listed below, this tireless trio has recorded *Sharon, Lois and Bram's Elephant Show Record* (1986), *Stay Tuned* (1987), and *Happy Birthday* (1988) on Elephant Records.

One Elephant, Deux Elephants (1978)
Elephant Records
P.O. Box 101, Station Z
Toronto, Ontario, Canada M5N 2Z3
Distributed in the U.S. by A&M Records
1416 N. LaBrea Ave.
Hollywood, CA 90028
Format: Cassette, LP, CD
Age Appeal: All ages
Target Ages: 4–8
Material: Inventive potpourri including traditional, international, and music-hall songs
Vocals: Sharon Hampson, Lois Lilienstein, Bram Morrison
Vocal Style: Three expressive, high-energy vocalists weave their voices into smooth, soaring harmonies
Instrumentation: Guitars, piano, percussion, strings, horns, and woodwinds

Highlights of this fresh and energetic album include "Cookie Jar," "Comin' Round the Mountain," "Tingalayo," "Candy Man," "Salty Dog," "Turkey in the Straw," and "Skinnamarink."

Smorgasbord (1979)
Elephant Records
(See *One Elephant, Deux Elephants* above for details.)

One of their strongest recordings. Highlights include "Peanut Butter," "Jenny Jenkins," "Three Little Monkeys," "Sur le pont," " 'A' You're Adorable," "Rags," and "Hey Dum."

Singing and Swinging (1980)
Elephant Records
(See *One Elephant, Deux Elephants* above for details.)

More wonderful songs. Highlights include "Charlie over the Ocean," "The Ants Go Marching," "The Muffin Man," "The Cat Came Back," "Monte sur un éléphant," "The Aba Daba Honeymoon," and "Precious Friends."

In the Schoolyard (1981)
Elephant Records
(See *One Elephant, Deux Elephants*, page 167, for details.)

Yet another collection of singable songs. Highlights include "Small World," "La Bamba," "Pufferbellies," "Rattlin' Bog," "Thumbkin," "Un Eléphant," "Tall Silk Hat," and "Down in the Valley."

One, Two, Three, Four, Look Who's Coming Through the Door! (1982)
Elephant Records
(See *One Elephant, Deux Elephants*, page 167, for details.)

Highlights include "Old Texas," "Shanty Medley," "Side by Side," "If I Could Have a Windmill," "La Bastringue," "Apple Picker's Reel," and "Jada."

Mainly Mother Goose (1984)
Elephant Records
(See *One Elephant, Deux Elephants*, page 167, for details.)

Ideal for listeners from two and a half to four years. Offerings include "Humpty Dumpty," "Move Over," "Simple Simon," "Miss Muffet/The Eensy Weensy Spider," and "Riding and Marching."

Nancy Silber and Tony Soll

Dinosaurs, Dolphins and Dreams: Songs from Bank Street (1984)
CMS Records
226 Washington St.
Mount Vernon, NY 10553
Format: Cassette, LP
Age Appeal: 5–7
Material: Thoughtful, upbeat songs addressing a variety of concerns and experiences of elementary-age children

Vocals: Nancy Silber and Tony Soll with backup chorus including children
Vocal Style: Folk-rock
Instrumentation: Guitars, keyboards, flute, percussion

Singer-songwriters Nancy Silber and Tony Soll created this cheerful recording when they worked together at the innovative Bank Street College of Education in New York City. With a warm rock sound that harks back to the sixties, Silber and Soll's songs are perceptive and optimistic.

Highlights include "Dinosaur Dreams," which stands up for the value of dreams; "Be Happy Now," a calypso-style plea for appreciating the good things in one's life; "The Cold," a cheerful acceptance of coping with the misery of a cold; "For Lack of Space (Throw It Out)," which describes with humor the process of thinning out one's possessions; and "Skipping Stones," a strong, singable rock song that celebrates this satisfying activity.

Paul Strausman

Camels, Cats and Rainbows (1982)
A Gentle Wind
P.O. Box 3103
Albany, NY 12203
Format: Cassette
Target Ages: 2–5
Material: Original and traditional songs for preschoolers
Vocals: Paul Strausman with harmony backup and children's chorus
Vocal Style: Warm, friendly, and melodious
Instrumentation: Guitars, flute, mandolin

A former day care teacher, performer Paul Strausman has assembled an award-winning recording which contains warm, humorous, and loving songs about animals and activities that encourage preschoolers to sing, dance, and pretend. This is an ideal recording for families and classroom groups who, already fans of Raffi, are ready to expand into new yet contiguous music.

Highlights include "Play My Drum," "The Season Song," "One Bottle Pop," "You Are My Sunshine," "The Ants Go Marching," "Emil, the Camel," "One Meatball," and "Cats."

Sweet Honey in the Rock

Internationally acclaimed Sweet Honey in the Rock interweave their powerful voices in dynamic a cappella harmonies. A five-woman group, Sweet Honey in the Rock have long performed for adult audiences. With *All for Freedom* they offer family audiences descriptions of how their music, influenced by the sounds of eighteenth- and nineteenth-century congregational singing, has been developed by African-Americans in the twentieth century.

Sweet Honey in the Rock director Bernice Johnson Reagon, a scholar of African-American children's lore from the South, and group members Aisha Kahlil and Nitanju Bolade Casel conduct workshops and live performances for younger audiences. For booking information, contact Roadwork, Inc., 1475 Harvard St. NW, Washington, D.C. 20009

All for Freedom (1989)
Music for Little People
P.O. Box 1460
Redway, CA 95560
Format: Cassette, LP, CD
Age Appeal: All ages
Target Ages: 4–8
Material: A celebration of the roots and future of African-American culture; words included
Vocals: Bernice Johnson Reagon, Evelyn Maria Harris, Ysaye Maria Barnwell, Aisha Kahlil, Nitanju Bolade Casel, and students from the Adam Elementary School Singers
Vocal Style: Superb a cappella
Instrumentation: Unique percussion

With elegantly textured songs and stories, *All for Freedom* is a stunning musical tribute to the roots, struggles, and successes of African-Americans. Sweet Honey members offer narrative explanations of the origins of their music which enhance the depth of the recording for listeners of all ages and of all cultures. This recording is a must-have for people who cherish the musical diversity of our country.

Every selection is a winner. The list includes "So Glad I'm Here," "Cumbayah," "Down in the Valley Two by Two," "The Little Shekere," "The Little Red Caboose," "All for Freedom," "Juba," "Everybody Ought to Know," "Calypso Freedom,"

"Amen," "Ise Oluwa," "Meeting at the Building," "Johanna and Rhody," "Make New Friends," "Horse and Buggy," "Silvie," and "Alunde and the Story of Ono."

Marlo Thomas and Friends

Free to Be . . . You and Me (1972)
Arista Records
6 W. 57th St.
New York, NY 10019
Format: Cassette, LP
Age Appeal: 5 and up
Material: Stories, songs, and poems celebrating the world of possibility and uniqueness; illustrated lyrics included
Vocals: Marlo Thomas and friends, including Mel Brooks, Billy De Wolfe, Harry Belafonte, Rosey Grier, Dick Cavett, Carol Channing, Alan Alda, Diana Ross, and Tom Smothers.
Instrumentation: Full sound

Marlo Thomas produced this ground-breaking recording as a gift for her niece, and ultimately for all children, to help them "feel free to be who they are and who they want to be." The album was revolutionary when it was first released back in 1972, and its positive messages of self-worth shared through music, poetry, and humor still sound fresh and alive.

Highlights include "Free to Be . . . You and Me," with the New Seekers; "Boy Meets Girl," with Mel Brooks and Marlo Thomas; "When We Grow Up," with Diana Ross; "Parents Are People," with Harry Belafonte and Marlo Thomas; "It's All Right to Cry," with Rosey Grier; "William's Doll," with Alan Alda; and "Atalanta," with Alan Alda and Marlo Thomas.

Free to Be . . . A Family (1988)
A&M Records
1416 N. LaBrea Ave.
Hollywood, CA 90028
Format: Cassette, LP
Age Appeal: 6 and up
Material: Stories, songs, and poems that describe contemporary family life, in-

cluding family structures and roles, adoption, learning to think independently, and articulating fears

Vocals: Marlo Thomas and friends, including Steve Martin, the Fat Boys, Soul Asylum, Pat Benatar, Amy Grant, Robin Williams, Lily Tomlin, Carly Simon, and other contemporary stars, with children's chorus.

Vocal Style: Eclectic contemporary

Instrumentation: Full sound

This glittering recording will help every family member thrive in our contemporary world. Through humor, music, and poetry served up by a dazzling array of performers, listeners are helped to appreciate that "each family is the right kind of family if it knows how to nourish, nurture, and love its children."

Highlights include "Boy Meets Girl . . . Again," with Mel Brooks and Marlo Thomas; "Something for Everyone," with Marlo Thomas, Kermit the Frog, and the Muppets; "Some Things Don't Make Any Sense at All," with Steve Martin; "It's Not My Fault," with Soul Asylum; "I'm Never Afraid (to Say What's on My Mind)," with Bonnie Raitt; "Doris Knows," with Whoopi Goldberg; "The Day Dad Made Toast," with Robin Williams; "Thank Someone," with Amy Grant and John Hiatt; "Yourself Belongs to You," with the Fat Boys; "And Superboy Makes Three," with Christopher Reeve, Elaine May, Mike Nichols, and Phil Donahue; "And That's the Truth," with Lily Tomlin; "The Stupid Song," with Ladysmith Black Mambazo; "Another Cinderella," with Marlo Thomas, Bea Arthur, Jane Curtin, and Gilda Radner; and "Turn of the Tide," with Carly Simon.

Tickle Tune Typhoon

Tickle Tune Typhoon's fresh, powerful vocals and instrumentation reflect a broad range of cross-cultural influences, including rock, folk, and Latin rhythms. Masterfully performing with flute, saxophone, synthesizer, and an assortment of stringed and percussion instruments, it blends sounds, rhythms, and ideas together in a big pot and adds a healthy helping of fun and humor.

The group's lyrics speak with love and enthusiasm to people of all ages, in all sizes, colors, and conditions. With songs written and arranged by group members Dennis Westphall, Lorraine Bayes, and Danny Deardorff, they focus on messages we all need to hear repeatedly: let's feel good about ourselves no matter what our shape, physical abilities, or family situation; let's celebrate our world and our lives together. This may all sound impossibly sappy, but it's not. These people have a very light touch.

Formed in 1980 as a four-member folk group, Tickle Tune Typhoon has grown to include eight musicians and an array of guest artists and costumed dancers and often collaborates with other performance organizations, including the Northwest Chamber Orchestra, the Zuva African Marimba Band, and the Kaleidoscope Children's Dance Company. Presently Tickle Tune Typhoon tours the West Coast, with an occasional visit to the East. While it's a big show to move around, this group is on its way to the top. We're going to be hearing a lot more from Tickle Tune Typhoon, whether on a local stage or on our TV screens.

For those of us out of range of its live performances, Tickle Tune Typhoon's recordings are a fabulous experience in their own right. At this writing, Tickle Tune Typhoon has produced four sensational albums and a concert video. So where does one begin? Each Tickle Tune Typhoon album is a jewel, so start with the first, *Circle Around,* and move forward through *Hug the Earth* and *All of Us Will Shine.* For holiday cheer, listen to the newest, *Keep the Spirit.*

There's a lot to hear on Tickle Tune Typhoon albums. The music is full, and the lyrics brim with humor and meaning, very much in the tradition of American musical theater. To enhance the listening experience, each recording contains lyric sheets. After a few listenings, sit with your family and read the words together as they are performed. Because the language is sophisticated and sometimes hard to hear, adults will want to clarify for children words or phrases they might have missed or simply don't understand. Some of the puns, such as those in "The Sea Song" on *Hug the Earth,* are beyond compare. Songs such as "Everyone Is Differently Abled" and "My Body Belongs to Me," both on *All of Us Will Shine,* address timely and urgent topics that you will want to discuss with your children. Reading and talking together about the words will make subsequent listenings even more fun and stimulating as you add a dimension to music listening that you and your kids may have been missing if you've been living on a diet of Top 40 music.

Circle Around (1983)

Tickle Tune Typhoon Records
P.O. Box 15153
Seattle, WA 98115
Format: Cassette, LP
Age Appeal: 3 to adult

Target Ages: 5–8

Material: An impressive collection of original songs celebrating life and variety, written by members of the ensemble, and a sprinkling of innovatively delivered childhood classics

Vocals: Dennis Westphall, Lorraine Bayes, Danny Deardorff, Angie Bolton, Dan Schmitt

Vocal Style: Strong, expressive ensemble singing influenced by Broadway musical theater

Instrumentation: Guitars, piano, saxophone, synthesizer, harmonica, drums, congas, banjo, flutes

Circle Around offers rich, insightful music with a full, high-energy sound all its own. It's a carefully blended selection of songs and sounds, but many songs stand out as extraordinary.

"Muscle Music" has a smooth Latin melody which encourages listeners to get up and move while listening to humorous lyrics about muscles and what they do.

"Vega Boogie" makes it fun to just talk about vegetables. Each verse is sung by a different member of the band, who explains what vegetable he or she likes. The word groupings are so rhythmically fascinating that kids may walk around reciting them ("My name is Lorraine/ I like my lettuce romaine/ I like my mustard greens/ And my fresh green beans"). Who knows? Maybe the next step will be to actually *eat* them.

"Monster Song" tells the tale of a hairy, scary, unbearably ugly monster who helps children who refused to help him. Despite the tongue-in-cheek tone, the catchy, singable chorus delivers a message that needs to be said: "It doesn't matter what you look like/ It doesn't matter from where you came/ It doesn't matter if you're different/ I'm gonna help you just the same." It's affectingly and effectively sung from a wheelchair by paraplegic Danny Deardorff, the song's author and one of the prime movers of Tickle Tune Typhoon.

"Tree Dancing" is a wonderful example of Tickle Tune Typhoon's ability to meld styles within a song. Beginning with a swing sound, the music evolves, very much like the seasons, into a reedy, honky-tonk beat and then into a smooth waltz. The lyrics interweave rich tree images and puns that beckon the listener to move, think, and be like a tree.

"Sneakers" is a joyful, vivid song in which kids wearing sneakers have superpowers. Written by Dennis Westphall, who delivers the lead vocal with a wonderful

Bullwinkle-the-moose-style voice, it presents the notion, irresistible to kids, that their feet are where they find their strength.

Tickle Tune Typhoon's "Dinosaur Song" paints a "bigger than big, bigger than huge" picture of dinosaurs walking around the neighborhood. With his enchantingly versatile voice, Dennis Westphall first exhibits his fear of dinosaurs, then gradually overcomes it in favor of his fascination with their size. In the end, all he wants to do is go for a ride.

"Clap Your Hands" is a traditional children's tune usually reserved for the toddler set. Although it may seem like an odd addition to Tickle Tune Typhoon's sophisticated repertoire, what starts out as a gentle sing-along evolves into a real audience rouser that will tantalize the most discerning school-age listeners.

Although many people have recorded "Magic Penny," Malvina Reynolds's 1955 children's classic—and for good reason—Tickle Tune Typhoon's version is, as usual, sophisticated and rich.

"Circle Around," the closing track, is a simple, elegant interpretation of a Native American song sung a cappella with crisp, affecting harmonies. It's a real tribute to the skill of this group that they can successfully wind down to such a peaceful and satisfying finale.

Hug the Earth (1985)

Tickle Tune Typhoon Records
Format: Cassette, LP
Age Appeal: 5–adult
Target Ages: 7–11
Material: An impressive collection of original songs celebrating life in all forms, and a sprinkling of innovatively delivered childhood classics
Vocalists: Dennis Westphall, Lorraine Bayes, Danny Deardorff, Angie Bolton, Andy Blythe, Gary Hillaire
Vocal Style: Strong, expressive ensemble singing influenced by Broadway musical theater
Instrumentation: Guitars, piano, saxophone, synthesizer, Autoharp, timbales, fiddle, drums, congas, banjo, flutes

It was hard for me to imagine that I could love Tickle Tune Typhoon's next album, *Hug the Earth,* as much as *Circle Around,* but it happened. Maybe it was because my son was older and it appeared just in time to address his growing ability to absorb more of what it means to be a human being.

Hug the Earth is not better than *Circle Around*, but it's for a slightly older audience. The target-age designation for *Hug the Earth*, at seven to eleven, is slightly older than that for *Circle Around*, at five to eight. While younger children can certainly enjoy this recording, the "coolest" kids in the seven-to-eleven-year-old category are best equipped to pick up on the sophisticated concepts about equality and the environment that are described and reinforced throughout.

The cover alone is a gem: a startling photo collage that shows children in a lush green meadow reaching for the earth, which hovers above them; printed along the bottom is "A celebration of life through music and dance." It's a big claim— one you won't be able to substantiate until you've bought the recording and listened to it several times. But have no fear: these people deliver.

Tickle Tune Typhoon has created ear-catching, multileveled music intertwined with appealing lyrics that sing about the quality of life in a way that adults and children can enjoy and understand together. It's a brilliant accomplishment; and I hope that once adults hear these lyrics, they will begin to wonder, as I do, why so few Top 40 songwriters and performers strive for this kind of thing.

Songs of special note on this recording include "Got the Rhythm," with simple and compelling words enhanced by an intricate dance beat created with drums, flute, and vocals; "Skin," with lyrics that say, "We are all the same relation/ Having different pigmentation"—the most articulate yet playful credo of human equality I've ever heard (if adults and kids have to pull out the dictionary together to define some of the words, that will be a wonderful activity too); "Doin' the Robot," with its video-game rhythms and effects that will capture the attention of kids who perk up at the sound of electronics; "Kye Kye Kule," an African call-and-response song that the Tickle Tune Typhooners deliver with infectious energy and spirit; "Sea Song," with salty puns and word plays ("I'm urchin you/ To look into the ocean blue . . ."), enhanced by an assortment of watery gurgles and echoes (while "Sea Song" may float over the heads of preschool children, it amuses and stimulates elementary-age listeners, especially those who are studying the marine environment in school); "Place in the Choir," a charismatic fantasy about the sounds animals would make if they joined together to sing, a contemporary masterpiece that makes a strong case for the importance of individuals contributing to society according to their abilities; "Super Kids," which offers children techniques for reaffirming their own power and effectiveness in an overbearing world; "If You're Happy," a traditional children's song in which Tickle Tune Typhoon pulls out the rug by encouraging listeners to sing about being mad and sad; "Garbage Blues," with silly yet graphic images of smelly garbage that send a strong message; "Family Song," written by Uncle Ruthie, a contemporary treasure that offers a positive and realistic picture of today's family groupings; "Hug the Earth," which describes the cycles of nature that produce clean air, food, and water for the world; and, finally, the haunting "Oh Cedar Tree," performed with Gary Hillaire, a Pacific Northwest Lummi Native American, who learned the chant at the bedside of his grandfather, who urged him to pass on the lore of the tree to all children so they would understand its value. It's an eloquent tribute to a tree, whose many beautiful parts have been indispensible to the lives of many people—a fitting closing for an elegant recording.

All of Us Will Shine (1987)

Tickle Tune Typhoon Records
Format: Cassette, LP
Age Appeal: 5–adult
Target Ages: 7–11
Material: Another impressive collection of original songs celebrating life in all forms, and a sprinkling of innovatively delivered childhood classics
Vocals: Lorraine Bayes, Danny Deardorff, Angie Bolton, Dennis Westphall
Vocal Style: Strong, expressive ensemble singing influenced by Broadway musical theater
Instrumentation: Guitars, piano, saxophone, synthesizer, mandolin, Autoharp, timbales, fiddle, drums, congas, banjo, flutes

This innovative group has created a third splendid album, and again the target age is seven to eleven. This doesn't mean that three-year-olds won't enjoy the fabulous music of *All of Us Will Shine;* but whereas a seven-year-old might want to talk about "bicuspids" and the many other teeth named in "Pearly White Waltz," a younger child might be overwhelmed by such a long string of unfamiliar words. On the other hand, how can a child's vocabulary grow if she isn't exposed to the richness of language?

Of particular note is the remarkable song written by Danny Deardorff called "Everyone Is Differently Abled." Powerfully articulating our need to focus on and celebrate the spectrum of human abilities, it is exquisitely performed by Deardorff, Tickle Tune Typhoon's talented ensemble member, producer, and arranger. Additional titles on this rich and satisfying album are "Let's Be Friends," "Flowers," "East/West," "Let the Sun Shine Forever," "Fine Wind Blowing," "My Body Belongs to Me," "Bicycle Cowboy," "Hokey Pokey," "We've Got the Whole World in our Hands," and "Twinkle, Twinkle, Little Star."

Stephen Tosh

The music performed by Stephen Tosh on *Lullabies from Around the World* and *Child's Play* is both surprising and satisfying. Sometimes reminiscent of a sophisticated music box, other times of a calliope, a harpsichord, a xylophone, a harp, or chimes, the sound is melodious, multilayered, and mellow.

Lullabies from Around the World (1986)
Troubadour Records
P.O. Box 6543
Carmel, CA 93921
Format: Cassette
Age Appeal: All ages
Target Ages: Newborn–6
Material: Traditional lullabies from around the world, including England, Germany, Sweden, Portugal, Africa, and Czechoslovakia
Vocals: none
Instrumentation: DX7 synthesizer, creating the sounds of bells, chimes, harps, flutes, and wood blocks
Musician: Stephen Tosh

Beyond citing the country of origin, Stephen Tosh does not identify the material on *Lullabies from Around the World,* and it is the delicate musicality rather than the selection of music that makes this a lullaby recording. Because only a handful of the selections are instantly identifiable as lullabies, parents may want to consider playing this recording for older children who are put off when they hear obvious "good night" music. Or they may want to play it at other times of day to help create a cheerful, optimistic ambience.

Child's Play (1987)
Troubadour Records
Format: Cassette
Age Appeal: All ages
Target Ages: Newborn–6
Material: Traditional nursery rhymes and songs of childhood
Vocals: none
Instrumentation: DX7 synthesizer, creating the sounds of bells, chimes, harps, flutes, and wood blocks
Musician: Stephen Tosh

This persistently cheerful instrumental recording may be just a bit upbeat to qualify as a lullaby collection. On the other hand, it may prove a wonderful tool for helping both adults and children survive those all-too-frequent cranky times of day.

   Among the nearly twenty songs, highlights include "Sing a Song of Sixpence," "Twinkle, Twinkle, Little Star," "Dance of the Sugar Plum Fairy," "Hickory Dickory Dock," and "Yankee Doodle Dandy."

Paul Tracey

The Rainbow Kingdom (1985)
A Gentle Wind
Box 3103
Albany, NY 12203
Format: Cassette
Target Ages: 4–7
Material: Imaginative, humorous original songs
Vocals: Paul Tracey with backup harmonies
Vocal Style: Elegant and sunny, influenced by musical theater
Instrumentation: Guitar, mandolin, percussion, flute, xylophone, tuba

This award-winning recording has a gentle charm and wit that reflects the quirky, theatrical sensibility of singer-songwriter Paul Tracey. A co-author of the international hit stage musical *Wait a Minim!*, Tracey began writing songs for children when his daughter was born.

   Songs of special note include "Rainbow Kingdom," with its rich imagery about colors and singable tune; "I Found It in a Book," a delightful ode to reading and libraries that deserves to become an international anthem; "Yukky," with its quick and effective changes between the pastoral and the gross; and "Fairy Godfather," in which Paul nearly squanders three wishes.

Troubadour

For gentle yet provocative listening with your family or students, seek out the recordings of Troubadour, whose carefully crafted images and ideas reflect a genuine understanding of the pleasures and conflicts of childhood. While the duo's energetic, tuneful songs and poems make listeners laugh or smile and tap their toes, the lyrics offer a lot to hear, think about, and discuss.

Victor Cockburn is the folklorist, Judith Steinbergh the poet of the team. In addition to their three childhood-focused recordings as Troubadour, Cockburn and Steinbergh record songs and poems for adults as well as publish poetry and a newsletter describing their activities, which interweave poetry and music. Two additional Troubadour recordings for children are *Are We Almost There?* and *Can We Go Now?*, both on A Gentle Wind.

As Troubadour and as solo performers, Cockburn and Steinbergh give in-school concerts and conduct workshops to help teachers enhance their classroom curricula with poetry and folk music. For more information, contact Troubadour through Judith Steinbergh at the address below.

Troubadour: Original Songs and Poems for Children (1983)
Troubadour Productions
99 Evans Road
Brookline, MA 02146
Format: Cassette
Age Appeal: 5–9
Material: Gentle, intelligent songs and poems about childhood, written with and for elementary-age schoolchildren
Vocals: Victor Cockburn and Judith Steinbergh; fifth graders from the Driscoll School
Vocal Style: Folk
Instrumentation: Guitars, banjo, percussion

"There's a Werewolf Under My Bed" is the standout favorite on this album. While the elaborate spooky-house sounds and the rousing, singable chorus make it fun for kids to hear, its well-deserved popularity is a result of how Troubadour uses its light touch to describe some of the realities that haunt our children. Too many horror movies and too many murders on the evening news *do* undermine our children's feelings of well-being. Our sophisticated children may not be able to express these fears easily, yet discussion is important. By interpreting "There's a Werewolf Under My Bed" as humorous or realistic, depending on the age and the needs of the child, adults can open up important dialogue with the children in their lives.

Additional highlights of this recording include "Who Am I?," a poem by sixth-grader Caitlin Pessin; "What Kids Are Supposed to Do," an upbeat, compassionate song describing the fears, difficulties, and indignities of struggling to overcome new and seemingly impossible challenges: learning to ride a bike, learning to roller skate, learning to swim; "Friends," which talks about the different ways that friendship endures; three short poems entitled "Spring," "Balloon," and "Rolling"; "Dying to Be Dirty," depicting how some kids revel in their dirt, asking for parents to accept them for who they are, not what they look like; "Fable," a poem that describes the bitter conflicts between a brother and sister and the frustrations of being their mother; "It's Not Fair!," an upbeat companion song to "Fable," which describes the inequities experienced by siblings; and "Wilderness," written and sung with fifth graders from the Driscoll School, Brookline, Massachusetts, a gentle, timely song about taking action to save our forests.

Uncle Ruthie

For nearly twenty years Uncle Ruthie has been playing music and telling stories for kids on her L.A.-based radio show, "Halfway Down the Stairs." With a special reverence for the virtues of radio listening, songwriter, singer, actress, and special education teacher Ruthie Buell chose her name to make fun "of all those other radio uncles, like Uncle Bob and Uncle Ben, who patronize children." In direct contrast, Uncle Ruthie is honest, loving, and respectful of children's needs and feelings.

With a strong belief that parents must actively deny their children access to the violence of television, she offers her radio programming as a sane alternative to Saturday-morning cartoons. "I try to build some gentleness into our society," she has said. If you are not within receiving range of 90.7 FM, KPFK in Los Angeles, you can share the nurturing, innovative music of Uncle Ruthie with your children by listening together to her recording *Take a Little Step*.

Uncle Ruthie, who has worked extensively in schools, hospitals, and mental health facilities, also gives concerts for kids and their families. In addition, she conducts workshops for parents and teachers in which she demonstrates how they can weave music and movement as well as storytelling into their classrooms and their family lives. In keeping with many educational leaders, Uncle Ruthie wants teachers to feel comfortable integrating music into the classroom throughout the day rather than have it "just be relegated to a period called 'music' or 'rhythms.' " Whether she is gearing the workshop to "special ed" or regular ed, Uncle Ruthie believes *all* education must be special.

Take a Little Step (1984)

Uncle Ruthie Buell
1731 S. Sherbourne Dr.
Los Angeles, CA 90035
Format: Cassette, LP
Age Appeal: All ages
Target Ages: 3–5
Material: Tuneful music and intelligent, thought-provoking lyrics that enhance the development of positive self-image and appreciation of others; all songs by Uncle Ruthie; lyric and activity sheet included
Vocals: Uncle Ruthie, Marcia Berman, Dave Zeitlin
Vocal Style: Gentle and melodic
Instrumentation: Piano, spoons, violin, guitar, accordion

Uncle Ruthie writes and sings eloquently about loving, supportive physical and emotional communication between people. In a time when many songs are being created to help children cope with physical and sexual abuse, the gentle, positive, occasionally startling songs about human needs on *Take a Little Step* are the perfect vehicles for helping children discover the loving side of their lives.

Accompanying this recording is a lyric and activity sheet on which Uncle Ruthie notes that all of side 1 and "The Goodbye Song" on side 2 are especially appropriate to classroom and group activity. The rest of the songs on side 2 are for listening and seeing.

Song highlights include "Party Song," which assures children that everyone is important; "Person Next to You," a vehicle for helping group members feel included; "Wake Up, Toes," in which listeners can enjoy moving different parts of their bodies; "Take a Little Step," written by Uncle Ruthie to encourage a child in a state hospital to learn to walk, which tells all people that life is filled with a combination of small steps; "The Very Best People," a sing-along to help children cope with those who think they are just a bit better than everyone else; "The Super Song," subtitled "The Non-Contingent Reinforcement Song," geared to help parents appreciate their kids not for their accomplishments but just for "being"; and "The Family Song," Uncle Ruthie's masterpiece about overcoming stereotyping.

Bill Usher

Most of us don't realize the debt we owe Bill for the ground-breaking children's recordings he produced back in 1977. By engineering the sound on the pioneer recordings of Sharon, Lois and Bram, Raffi, and ROSENSHONTZ, Bill showed the world that child-oriented music could be sophisticated, intelligent, and fun for listeners of all ages.

Bill's innovative vision for family-oriented recordings came into focus while he played drums on the rock music circuit and began his own family. In 1981, with a very clear philosophy that global peace begins at home, he started Kids' Records in Toronto. Kids' Records developed a diverse list of more than forty recordings that provide families with an exciting assortment of positive musical sounds that both entertain and empower listeners.

While Kids' Records productions delivered the kind of full, sophisticated sound that appeals to our media-savvy children, couched in the high-level productions were universal yet rarely articulated issues. Rather than lyrics about unrequited love and the glory of drugs enhanced by the rock beat, the words on Kids' Records productions were relevant to our changing world: how we can bring peace to our lives by feeling good about ourselves and others; how and why we should overcome sexual and racial stereotyping; and how we can and must find creative solutions to resolving conflicts and learn to appreciate today's blended families.

The superb recordings by Kids' Records, including those of Bob McGrath, Kim and Jerry Brodey, and Sally Rogers, are now distributed nationwide by a variety of organizations.

Drums (1986)
Golden Music
Western Publishing
1220 Mound Ave.
Racine, WI 53404
Format: Cassette, LP
Age Appeal: 6 and up
Material: Personal overview of the sounds of drumming, with percussion styles including African drumming, Bo Diddley–type rock 'n' roll, New Orleans jazz, and high-tech rap
Vocals: Bill Usher with ensemble accompaniment
Vocal Style: Vocal and instrumental selections in a variety of musical styles, tied together and enhanced by autobiographical narration
Instrumentation: Dozens of rhythm instruments from around the world

An intimate and charismatic introduction to the many facets of drumming, Bill Usher's recording (written in collaboration with Robert Morgan) stands alone in its category. It is ideal for all listeners who, like Bill, are irresistibly drawn to the sound and activity of drumming. In addition to the musical selections, which are rich and satisfying, Bill has added an unexpected layer of autobiographical narration, including fascinating descriptions of his own musical experiences and creative process.

Beginning with a military roll of the snare drum, the recording moves into a rock 'n' roll tribute to Bo Diddley. Highlights of the recording include "Drums Rapped in Time," a rap-style description of what happens to the drum in the recording studio, complete with appropriate sound effects and a large helping of vocabulary-building words like "oscillate" and "reverberate"; "Scatting with Some Garbage Can," in which Bill describes how his drumming drove his parents and teachers crazy; "Brothers," a love letter to the radio; "Haitian Playground Chant" and "Haitian Ra Ra," about Bill's musical adventures in Haiti (the first describes visiting a school, where he records the children singing; the second details going out into the night to play his newly purchased drum and being joined by local musicians); "I Go Down to Carnival," describing the birth of calypso music and how it melded with rock 'n' roll to create the sounds of Soca; and "Highlife Finale," in which Bill tells how the Bo Diddley beat came from Africa. Using it, he stresses the importance of listening: broadcasting and receiving, giving and taking. These are musical references with universal implications.

Michele Valeri and Michael Stein

Dinosaur Rock (1983)
Caedmon
10 E. 53rd St.
New York, NY 10022
Format: Cassette, LP
Target Ages: 5–9
Material: An original, high-energy rock opera for children
Vocals: Michele Valeri and Michael Stein
Vocal Style: Rock-country mix
Instrumentation: Guitars, piano, drums, tuba, fiddle, banjo, mandolin, concertina

Composed and performed by Michele Valeri and Michael Stein, *Dinosaur Rock* is the story of what happens when two children meet Professor Jones, a paleontologist with the power to bring dinosaurs temporarily back to life. This tall tale is laced with high-energy music that is simultaneously entertaining and informative. Skillfully delivered in a mix of styles including fifties rock 'n' roll, folk-rock, and country, *Dinosaur Rock* will appeal to kids and their parents who enjoy a full sound in their music and happen to love dinosaurs as well.

Songs included on this satisfying, fast-paced recording are: "The Dinosaur Song," "Professor Jones," "Dinosaur Rock," "Stella Stegosaurus," "The Sauropod Swing," "Tyrannosaurus Rex," "The Tiny Little Babies and the Great Big Momma," "The Hadrasaur from Hackensack," "Leapin Lizards," "Where Did Everybody Go?," and "We All Came from the Sea."

In 1984 *Dinosaur Rock* was transformed into a touring stage production. With the story adjusted slightly, Michele Valeri and Michael Stein perform the songs with energy and enthusiasm. The dinosaurs are portrayed with artistry and good humor by award-winning puppeteer Ingrid Crepeau.

Jim Valley

Jim Valley spent the 1960s performing with rock 'n' roll bands, including Paul Revere and the Raiders. For the last ten years, however, he has been conducting songwriting workshops at elementary schools in the Northwest, and that's what he likes best.

Booked a year in advance, Jim estimates that he works with about twenty-five thousand kids a year. "I ask myself, would I rather be in Reno playing with the Raiders?" he has said. "It isn't even close. This is a dream job. . . . Kids have messages adults need to hear. I think there's an amazing depth in children that we don't see."

Now a grandfather, Jim aims to teach children how to accomplish their goals through cooperation and friendship. His recordings are distinguished by their bouncy, cozy sound and optimistic concepts.

The songs on Jim's recordings pair the lyrics created by kids during these sessions (for which the schools receive royalties) with music that Jim composes, reflecting his rock 'n' roll roots. "Rock is intrinsically happy," he has said. "Good ol' rock 'n' roll songs lend themselves to a positive attitude." Included on each of his children's recordings is at least one classic, such as Bobby Darin's "Splish Splash" and Chuck Berry's "Johnny B. Goode."

Additional recordings by Jim Valley include *Friendship Train*, *Imagine That!*, and *Dinosaur Ride*.

Rainbow Planet (1984)
Rainbow Planet
P.O. Box 735
Edmonds, WA 98020
Format: Cassette
Age Appeal: All ages
Target Ages: 4–8
Material: Sweet, mostly original lyrics written by schoolchildren about friendship and fantasy, coupled with accomplished, bouncy rock 'n' roll music
Vocals: Jim Valley, with children and adults
Vocal Style: Friendly and infectious
Instrumentation: Electric guitars, piano, DX7 keyboard, synthesizer, drums, percussion

Rainbow Planet is focused on caring for people and the importance of appreciating and nurturing individual differences. Warm and cheerful, this is a recording that some children may want to hear repeatedly.

Jim has published the *Rainbow Planet* songbook to accompany the recording; it provides teachers with the music and lyrics and suggestions for related activities that can be adapted to many grade levels.

Highlights include "Rainbow Planet," "The Computer Song," "How Could I Change the World," "Penguins," "Splish Splash," "Bones," and "Unicorn Song."

The Weavers

With Pete Seeger's blazing banjo, Fred Hellerman's virtuoso Spanish guitar, and spectacular vocal harmonies (Ronnie Gilbert and Lee Hays completed the foursome), the Weavers introduced traditional and international folk music to middle-class America. Formed in 1948, the Weavers created their own innovative sound that was simultaneously exhilarating, inspiring, down-to-earth, and earth shaking. By the 1950s they had earned national acclaim with their hit songs "Goodnight Irene," "On Top of Old Smokey," and "So Long, It's Been Good to Know You."

Carl Sandburg has said: "The Weavers are the grass roots of America. I salute them for their great work in authentic renditions of ballads, folk songs, ditties, nice antiques of words and melody. When I hear America singing, the Weavers are there."

While they no longer perform together as a group, their glorious ensemble music lives on, the seminal influence of many now-familiar performers, including Peter, Paul and Mary, Sharon, Lois and Bram, and Tom Chapin. Still fresh and pungent in sound and attitude, Weavers recordings make great family listening.

I grew up listening to the Weavers, and I made sure my son did too. Younger children and their parents can appreciate the soaring vocals, sparkling accompaniments, and infectious rhythms. Elementary-age children, with their parents or teachers, can experience curriculum subjects coming alive. "Wasn't That a Time," "Two Brothers," "Follow the Drinking Gourd," "Greenland Fisheries," "Study War No More," and "If I Had a Hammer" can be directly related to lessons about American history, war, peace, and brotherhood.

The Weavers on Tour (1958)

Vanguard Records
A Welk Record Group Company
Santa Monica, CA 90401
Format: Cassette, LP
Material: Traditional and original songs of America and the world
Age Appeal: All ages
Vocals: Pete Seeger, Ronnie Gilbert, Lee Hays, and Fred Hellerman
Vocal Style: Soaring, inventive two- and three-part harmonies and ensemble singing
Instrumentation: Long-necked banjo, twelve-string guitar, Spanish guitar, recorder

Songs on this magnificent album include "Tzena, Tzena," "On Top of Old Smokey," "Drill Ye Tarriers, Drill," "Fi-li-mi-oo-ree-ay," "Over the Hill," "Clementine," "The Frozen Logger," "The Boll Weevil," "Talking Blues," "I Don't Want to Get Adjusted," "So Long, It's Been Good to Know You," "Michael, Row the Boat Ashore," "The Wreck of the 'John B'," "Two Brothers (The Blue and the Grey)," "Ragaputi," "Wasn't That a Time," "Go Tell It on the Mountain," "Poor Little Jesus," "Mi Y'Malel," "Santa Claus Is Coming (It's Almost Day)," and "We Wish You a Merry Christmas."

The Weavers' Greatest Hits (1982)

Vanguard Records
(See *The Weavers on Tour* above for details.)

The equivalent of two long-play records on one tape, this composite contains twenty-five Weavers classics, including "When the Saints Go Marching In," "Last Night I Had the Strangest Dream," "Wimoweh," "Follow the Drinking Gourd," "Wreck of the 'John B'," "Rock Island Line," "This Land Is Your Land," "Michael, Row the Boat Ashore," "If I Had a Hammer," and "So Long, It's Been Good to Know You."

"Weird Al" Yankovic

"Weird Al" Yankovic, rock 'n' roll's most outspoken parodist, has described himself as a man whose purpose in life is to "slam a stapler against the forehead of American pop culture." With multiple gold albums, a Grammy, an American Video Award, and many other accolades to his credit, he's succeeding in a big way.

"Weird Al" isn't going to appeal to everyone, but if yours is a family that appreciates *Mad* magazine–type humor, he is a person you can enjoy by listening together.

While an architecture student in California, Al Yankovic reshaped the hit song "My Sharona" into a raucous diatribe about his passion for eating bologna. The lyrics were clever and funny, and the music sounded like the original. As an added ingredient, Al's affinity for the vulgar inspired him to pepper the song lightly with well-placed belches. While the song hardly appeals to a discerning adult, my son at age eleven thinks that it is *the* funniest thing he has *ever* heard.

The music of "Weird Al" could never be labeled wholesome, yet I must admit that I have grown to appreciate the ingenious ways Al finds to turn a song inside out, and Jesse enjoys the intrinsic humor and the skillful, high-energy sound of the music. Best of all, I see that Al's outrageousness can encourage kids to question the world as they hear it depicted in Top 40 music.

With the uncanny knack of mimicking both vocal and instrumental styles, Al takes on the likes of Michael Jackson, George Harrison, Los Lobos, the Police, Billy Idol, Madonna, Huey Lewis, and the Kinks. While Jesse is able to identify some of the songs that Al spoofs, he also enjoys many "Weird Al" songs without even knowing the originals.

The music and sensibility of "Weird Al" Yankovic is targeted to ten- to fourteen-year-old listeners, though many seven-year-olds will be attracted to his humor. Although a few of his high-energy creations tread a very thin line between the funny and the offensive, rather than pass up the opportunity to enjoy and benefit from Al's off-the-wall humor, be prepared to discuss openly with your children why you are offended by a particular song or attitude.

"Weird Al" Yankovic (1983)
Rock 'n' Roll Records/CBS
1801 Century Park West
Los Angeles, CA 90036
Format: Cassette, LP
Age Appeal: 9–14
Material: Irreverent spoofs of Top 40 hits
Vocals: "Weird Al" Yankovic
Vocal Style: Tongue-in-cheek reproduction of original
Instrumentation: Electric guitars, synthesizer, drums, accordion

Highlights include "Ricky," a parody of Toni Basil's blockbuster hit "Mickey"; "I Love Rocky Road," depicting Al's loyalty to this famous ice cream flavor; and "My Bologna," a love song to another favorite food.

"Weird Al" Yankovic in 3-D (1984)
Rock 'n' Roll Records/CBS
(See *"Weird Al" Yankovic*, page 189, for details.)

"Weird Al" Yankovic in 3-D was named comedy album of the year in 1984, and *People* magazine called it one of the year's ten best. Highlights include "Theme from Rocky XIII," "Eat It," and "I Lost on Jeopardy."

Even Worse (1988)
Rock 'n' Roll Records/CBS
(See *"Weird Al" Yankovic*, page 189, for details.)

The album cover of *Even Worse* is an ingenious parody of Michael Jackson's *Bad*. Highlights include "Fat," "(This Song's Just) Six Words Long," "You Make Me," and "Lasagna."

Peter and the Wolf (1988)
CBS Records
51 W. 52nd St.
New York, NY 10019
Format: Cassette, LP, CD
Target Ages: 10–14
Material: Traditional music with humorous narration
Vocals: Narrated by "Weird Al" Yankovic
Instrumentation: Arranged and performed by Wendy Carlos and the LSI Philharmonic

Keeping the music intact, "Weird Al" fractures the classic Prokofiev tale with humorous characterizations, off-beat narration, and rude sound effects. Many kids who shunned classical music will be drawn into Al's wacky world, humming Prokofiev's catchy themes long after the wolf gives his final belch.

The flip side contains a parody of Saint-Saëns's *Carnival of the Animals*, with music by Wendy Carlos and poems by "Weird Al."

Parents' Resource Guide

Children's Media Review Publications

The following publications review media for children and are available by subscription or in libraries.

Children's Video Report
145 W. 96th St., Suite 7C
New York, NY 10025-6403

Children's Video Report is designed to help parents, teachers, and librarians discriminate among the hundreds of videotapes on the market. Published six times a year, it contains reviews with age-group recommendations as well as articles about child development, critical viewing skills, and great ways to use tapes.

Parents' Choice
P.O. Box 185
Newton, MA 02168

An important watchdog children's media review publication, *Parents' Choice* is published four times a year, issuing annual awards each fall for excellence in audio, video, and publishing.

Kidsnet

6858 Eastern Ave. NW, Suite 208
Washington, D.C. 20012
(202) 291-1400

A computerized clearinghouse for children's television and radio, Kidsnet publishes a monthly newsletter for parents listing noteworthy upcoming television and radio programs for children.

Parenting Publications

While nationally distributed parenting magazines can address the broad issues of family life, regional parenting magazines and newspapers serve the needs of families at the local level. Usually published monthly, these publications feature calendars of local events as well as articles on regional activities, services, and people. Their commitment to disseminating regional information will inherently limit their growth, yet family-oriented publications have become invaluable resources within their communities. I urge all parents to seek out these local publications.

To pay their bills, parenting periodicals run classified and display ads for a host of family-related services, from birthday-party organizing to family counseling. This is the kind of information that tells parents what resources are available within their community.

In addition to the smallest neighborhood tabloids, thirty-five moderate-size regional magazines and newspapers have joined together in an innovative organization called Parenting Publications of America. Each member publication conforms to established standards, including print quality and frequency of publication. Circulation among members ranges from five thousand to one hundred thousand households per title; and with a combined circulation of over 1.5 million, these publications offer advertisers the opportunity to reach audiences across the country through one central office.

Parenting Publications of America

12715 Path Finder Lane
San Antonio, TX 78230
(512) 492-9057

The following list contains the names of member publications.

California

Bay Area Parent Newsmagazine
455 Los Gatos Blvd., Suite 103
Los Gatos, CA 95032
(408) 358-1414

L.A. Parent
P.O. Box 3204
Burbank, CA 91504
(818) 846-0400

Parenting Magazine
1905 E. 17 St., Suite 122
Santa Ana, CA 92701
(714) 550-1240

Parents' Press
1454 Sixth St.
Berkeley, CA 94710
(415) 524-1602

San Diego Family Press
P.O. Box 23960
San Diego, CA 92123
(619) 541-1162

San Diego Parent Magazine
2165 San Diego Ave., Suite 105
San Diego, CA 92110
(619) 574-1157

San Francisco Peninsula Parent
P.O. Box 89
Millbrae, CA 94030
(415) 342-9203

Colorado

The Parent Newspaper (formerly
Denver Parent)
818 East 19th Ave.

Denver, CO 80218
(303) 832-7822

Florida

The Mothers' Network
P.O. Box 1692
Pinellas Park, FL 34664
(813) 522-3175

Tampa Bay Parent
5700 Memorial Hwy., Suite 211
Tampa, FL 33615
(813) 889-0341

Georgia

Youth View Magazine
1401 West Paces Ferry Rd. NW,
   Suite A-217
Atlanta, GA 30327
(404) 231-0562

Illinois

Chicago Parent
7001 N. Clark St., #217
Chicago, IL 60626
(312) 508-0973

Indiana

Indy's Child
8888 Keystone Crossing, Suite 1050
Indianapolis, IN 46240
(317) 843-1494

Maryland

Baltimore's Child
11 Dutton Ct.
Catonsville, MD 21228
(301) 367-5883

Massachusetts
The Boston Parents' Paper
P.O. Box 1777
Boston, MA 02130
(617) 522-1515

Child's Play
401 Dickinson St.
Springfield, MA 01106
(413) 733-8055, ext. 10

Michigan
All Kids Considered
4000 Town Center, Suite 710
Southfield, MI 48075
(303) 352-0990

Grand Rapids Parents
Trust Building, Suite 1040
40 Pearl St. NW
Grand Rapids, MI 49503
(616) 459-4545

New Jersey
Suburban Parent
575 Cranbury Rd., Suite B5
East Brunswick, NJ 08816
(201) 390-0566

New York
The Big Apple Parents' Paper
67 Wall St., Suite 2411
New York, NY 10005
(212) 323-8070

New York Family
and
Westchester Family
420 East 79th St., Suite 9E

New York, NY 10021
(212) 744-0309

W.N.Y. Family
297 Parkside Ave.
Buffalo, NY 14215-0244
(716) 836-3486

Ohio
All About Kids
Department of Pediatrics
University of Cincinnati College of
    Medicine
Cincinnati, OH 45267-0541
(513) 558-4216

Considering Kids
P.O. Box 24-D
Cincinnati, OH 45224
(513) 521-6454

Pennsylvania
Pittsburgh's Child
Box 418
10742 Babcock Blvd.
Gibsonia, PA 15044
(412) 443-1891

SKIP
P.O. Box 404
Bala Cynwyd, PA 19004
(215) 664-1952 or 668-4000

Texas
Dallas Child
3330 Earhart Drive, #102
Carrollton, TX 75007
(214) 960-8474

Our Kids Houston
and
Our Kids San Antonio
6804 West Ave.
San Antonio, TX 78213
(512) 349-6667

Virginia
Wednesday's Child
P.O. Box 35612
Richmond, VA 23235
(804) 745-0498

Washington
Eastside Parent
and
Seattle's Child
P.O. Box 22578

Seattle, WA 98122
(206) 322-2594

Pierce County Parent
P.O. Box 98402
Tacoma, WA 98498
(206) 565-4004 or 847-7561

Washington, D.C.
Parent and Child
7048 Wilson Lane
Bethesda, MD 20817
(301) 229-2216

Canada: Ontario
Kids Toronto
542 Mt. Pleasant Road, #401
Toronto, Ont., Canada M4S 2M7
(416) 481-5696

Radio Programs for Children

Described on the following pages, organized in a state-by-state format, are radio shows for family listening that are broadcast on local radio stations across the United States. Signal strengths vary from station to station, so be sure to seek out programs listed under states within a fifty-mile radius of your home. My family lives in suburban New York more than fifty miles away from WFDU in Teaneck, New Jersey, yet "Imagination Parade" comes in loud and clear on the aqua plastic radio on our kitchen counter.

Not every station has such a strong signal. The better the radio, the more distant the signal it will pick up. You might discover that you have stronger reception on your car radio than you do on the radio in the bedroom. You can boost the reception range of your household radio dramatically by attaching it to a roof antenna.

Four shows on this list are in syndication and can be heard on independent stations across the country. Because they are aired in such diverse locations as Valdez, Alaska, and Panama City, Florida, read through the accompanying lists of stations to see what is broadcast in your area. Listed under their states of origin, programs to check include "We Like Kids" (Alaska) and "Pickleberry Pie" and "The Mind's Eye" (both California). "Knock on Wood" and "Kids Alive," two programs that originate in New York State, are expecting to be syndicated soon.

Also included in the following pages are a few pioneering shows that are now extinct. While no longer on the air, they deserve to be recognized for their important contributions to the quality of contemporary radio for children.

While single, independently produced programs for children remain spotty, there is growing interest in full-format satellite-broadcast radio stations for family audiences. At this writing it is likely that several family-oriented networks will emerge. Keep your ears open for Kids' Choice Broadcasting Network, WPRD, 1440 AM, Orlando, Florida, which plans to provide twenty-four hours of programming daily to eleven radio stations across the nation; The Children's Radio Network, WWTC, 1280 AM, Minneapolis, St. Paul, Minnesota; and Kidwaves Radio Network, 1207 Chestnut Street, Philadelphia, Pennsylvania 19107.

To be completely accurate, radio listings would have to be updated monthly. Since this is impossible in a book like *All Ears,* I will have to be content with telling you that at this writing, ours is the most complete information about radio programs for children that has ever been assembled. Special thanks go to Jamie Deming, producer of "Kids Alive," for her energy and enthusiasm in gathering this information. I encourage readers to keep us apprised of their own radio projects for future printings of *All Ears.* Wonderful new shows are being born every day.

Happy listening!

Alaska

"We Like Kids," produced at KTOO, 104.3 FM in Juneau, is a half-hour weekly program of music and stories for family listening. Hosted by Jeff, Judy, and Jan, this program is currently aired by more than twenty stations in the National Public Radio system.

Jeff Brown, Producer
224 4th St.
Juneau, AK 99801
(907) 586-1607

"We Like Kids" can be heard in:

Alaska

Barrow	KBRW 680 AM
Bethel	KYUK 640 AM
Chevak	KCUK 88.1 AM
Dillingham	KDLG 670 AM
Galena	KIYU 910 AM
Haines	KHNS 102.3 AM
Homer	KBBI 890 AM
Juneau	KTOO 104.3 FM
Ketchikan	KRBD 105.9 FM
Kodiak	KMXT 100.1 FM
Kotzebue	KOTZ 720 AM
McGrath	KSKO 870 AM
Petersburg	KFSK 100.9 FM
St. Paul Island	KUHB 91.9 AM
Sand Point	KSDP 840 AM
Sitka	KCAW 104.7 FM
Unalakleet	KNSA 930 AM
Unalaska	KIAL 1450 AM
Valdez	KCHU 770 AM
Wrangell	KSTK 101.7 FM

Arkansas

Jonesboro	KASU 91.9 FM

California

Arcata	KHSU 90.5 FM
San Francisco	KALW 91.7 FM
San Luis Obispo	KCBX 90.1 FM

Florida

Panama City	WKGC 90.7 FM

Kentucky

Louisville	WFPL 89.3 FM
Morehead	WMKY 90.3 FM

Michigan

Flint	WFBE 95.1 FM

Minnesota

Grand Rapids	KAXE 91.7 FM

Missouri

Columbia	KOPN 89.5 FM
Springfield	KSMU 91.1 FM
Warrensburg	KCMW 90.9 FM

Montana

Missoula	KUFM 89.1 FM

Oregon

Astoria	KMUN 91.9 FM
Portland	KBPS 1450 AM

Washington

Olympia	KAOS 89.9 FM

Wisconsin

Milwaukee	WYMS 88.9 FM

California

"Pickleberry Pie" is a half-hour weekly program for young children which is organized around themes such as making mistakes and animal moms. Hosted by Linda Arnold (see page 72), it also features the Pickleberries, a group of delicious, squeaky-voiced characters who are assigned the project of finding appropriate music. Produced in Santa Cruz, California, award-winning "Pickleberry Pie" has been syndicated by Longhorn Radio Network in Austin, Texas, for over three years and can be heard on many stations around the country. Prior to Linda Arnold, producer P. J. Swift hosted the program.

P. J. Swift, Producer
305 Dickens Way
Santa Cruz, CA 95064
(408) 427-3980

"Pickleberry Pie" can be heard in:

Illinois
Glen Ellyn   WDCB 90.9 FM

Indiana
Gary   WGVE 88.7 FM

Maryland
Frostburg   WFWM 91.5 FM

Michigan
Detroit   WDTR 90.9 FM

Missouri
Columbia   KOPN 89.5 FM

New York
Brockport   WBSU 88.9 FM
Brooklyn   WNYE 91.5 FM

Ohio
De Graff   WDEQ 91.1 FM

Pennsylvania
Clarion   WCUC 91.7 FM
York   WVYC 88.1 FM

South Dakota
St. Francis   KINI 96.1 FM

Virginia
Radford   WVRU 89.9 FM

"Pickleberry Pie" is also broadcast by satellite after "We Like Kids" (see listings on pages 197–198).

"The Mind's Eye" is a series of half-hour weekly radio dramas for kids six and up. Based on classics of children's literature (including *The Wizard of Oz*, *The Wind in the Willows*, and *Peter Pan*), these beautifully produced audio stories capture the imaginations of listeners of all ages. The series is distributed through the Longhorn Radio Network in Austin, Texas.

The Mind's Eye
4 Commercial Blvd.
Novato, CA 94947
(415) 883-7701

"The Mind's Eye" can be heard in:

Illinois
Glen Ellyn   WDCB 90.9 FM

Indiana
Gary   WGVE 88.7 FM
Goshen   WGCS 91.1 FM

Maryland
Princess Anne   WESM 91.3 FM

Michigan
Detroit   WDTR 90.9 FM

Nebraska
Lincoln   KZUM 89.3 FM

New York
Brockport   WBSU 88.9 FM
Brooklyn   WNYE 91.5 FM

North Carolina
Boiling Springs   WGWG 88.3 FM

Ohio
Hamilton   WHSS 89.5 FM

Pennsylvania
York   WVYC 88.1 FM

South Dakota
St. Francis   KINI 96.1 FM

Texas
Crockett   KIVY 1290 AM
San Antonio   KSYM 90.1 FM

Virginia
Radford   WVRU 89.9 FM

"The Little People Hour" is a live show of music, stories and interviews for pre-schoolers through fourth graders. It is aired Saturday mornings from 11:00 a.m. to noon on KSPC, 88.7 FM, Claremont, California.

"Halfway Down the Stairs" is produced and hosted by Uncle Ruthie (see page 181), songwriter, performer, and music educator. On the air for twenty years, "Halfway Down the Stairs" offers music and stories for young children. It is aired Saturdays, from 10:30 a.m. to 11:30 a.m., on KPFK, 90.7 FM, Los Angeles, California.

"The Storyteller" and "The Story Hour" alternate on Tuesdays at 7:00 p.m. for family audiences on KKUP, 91.5 FM, Cupertino, California.

Colorado

"Children's Rainbow" is a half-hour program of music and stories which airs live weekdays at 3:00 p.m. on KRZA, 88.7 FM, Alamosa, Colorado. Broadcasting in both English and Spanish, producer Fred Romero targets preschool and early-elementary-age students.

Indiana

Targeting elementary-age listeners, WETL, 91.7 FM, offers a variety of programs for children that focus on language arts, math, and science. They broadcast daily from 8:00 a.m. to 4:30 p.m.; a program guide is available.

Maine

"The Children's Hour," geared to six-to-twelve-year-old listeners, offers music, riddles, stories, and interviews with children who make public announcements about activities that are of interest to them and their families. This program is broadcast on Saturdays from 10:00 a.m. to 11:00 a.m. on WERU, 89.9 FM, Blue Hill Falls, Maine.

Massachusetts

"Children's Radio Space" airs Saturday mornings from 8:30 a.m. to 9:00 a.m. on WUMB, 91.9 FM, University of Massachusetts, Boston. Offering music and stories, this prerecorded program is designed for listeners from five to ten years old. In conjunction with this show, the station runs special picnics and concerts.

"Kid Company" is a live, interactive, issue-oriented talk show for eight-to-fourteen-year-old listeners. Featuring news spots written and produced by kids, opinion polls, a trivia quiz, celebrity interviews, a family therapist, radio drama by Bill Harley, music, and storytelling, it airs Sundays from 6:00 p.m. to 7:00 p.m. on WBZ, 1030 AM, Boston.

"Time for Young People" is a live program of music, stories, and interviews for children which airs on Saturdays from 9:00 a.m. to 11:00 a.m. and from 4:00 p.m. to 5:30 p.m. on WBRS, 91.7 FM, Waltham.

"Rainbow Tales" is a storytelling program which broadcasts once a week on WMBR, 88.1 FM, Cambridge. It is produced by Betty Lehrmann, editor of *LANES* (League for the Advancement of New England Storytelling) *Museletter.*

"The Sunday Morning Cereal Box," offering music and stories, targets children from five to twelve. It is broadcast on WRCA, 1330 AM, from 8:00 a.m. to 1:00 p.m., with host Joyce Quinlan.

Missouri

"New Generation Radio" is a term coined at radio station KOPN, 89.5 FM, Columbia, Missouri, to describe its remarkable commitment to programming for and by children. In addition to organizing hands-on workshops for kids at the radio station, director of children's programming Tina Hubbs arranges special days for kids to be on the air. Tina also runs conferences and workshops for adults, showing them how to involve children in audio projects in schools, camps, and at home.

Montana

"The Pea Green Boat" is a program of music, stories, book reviews, conversation, and commentary for children and their families. Hosted by Marcia Dunn, this award-winning program has been on the air for over ten years. Broadcast from the University of Montana in Missoula, it can be heard weekdays from 4:00 p.m. to 5:00 p.m. on KUFM, 89.1 FM.

"Children's Corner," KUFM, Missoula, is also produced and hosted by Marcia Dunn. Similar in format to "The Pea Green Boat," "Children's Corner" is aired Saturdays from 8:00 a.m. to 11:30 a.m.

New Jersey

"Imagination Parade" is an hour-and-a-half live show that airs early Sunday mornings on WFDU, 89.1 FM, Teaneck, New Jersey. Addressing younger children, host Paul Butler regularly announces listeners' birthdays, plays music, reads stories, and conducts interviews. He also encourages listeners to phone the show to respond to questions or request music.

New York

"Knock on Wood" is a weekly half-hour series of programs of music and stories for children ages three to ten. Woven into the text of the shows are drama and sound effects reminiscent of old-time radio. Produced and currently broadcast at WAMC, 90.3 FM, in Albany, New York, "Knock on Wood" is awaiting national syndication.

Steve Charney
WAMC
318 Central Ave.
Albany, NY 12260
(518) 465-5233

"Kids Alive" is an award-winning program of music and discussion co-hosted by children and producer Jamie Deming. Geared to listeners in kindergarten through fourth grade, "Kids Alive" addresses topics including messy rooms, procrastination, the environment, and friendships. Currently aired on Wednesdays from 5 p.m. to 6 p.m. at WCWP, 88.1 FM, on Long Island, Jamie expects "Kids Alive" to be syndicated to other stations in the near future.

Jamie T. Deming
Children's Radio Productions
Northern Blvd.
East Norwich, NY 11732
(516) 922-7307

"Kids America" (originally called "Small Things Considered"), a weekday hour-and-a-half program for primary-school kids, was on the air from 1984 to December 31, 1987. No list of children's radio programs would be complete without mention of this innovative, award-winning show. A fast-paced blend of listener-centered games, opinion polls, information, fantasy, music, and conversation, "Kids America" was produced by WNYC in New York City. Distributed on the American Public Radio network, it was carried by as many as twenty-six stations from 6:30 p.m. to 8:00 p.m. Eastern Time.

North Carolina

"East of the Sun, West of the Moon" was a series (not currently aired) of fifteen educational half-hour programs on American history and the humanities, covering topics including frontier days; kings, queens, and castles; and the presidency. John Lithgow was the host of this elaborately produced show.

Children's Audio Service
P.O. Box 4015
Chapel Hill, NC 27515
(919) 933-0300

North Dakota

"Kids World News" is a five-minute program of news and features of interest to children, airing Saturday mornings at 8:00 on KFNW, 1200 AM, in Fargo. Producer Shirley Bevier presents material for children from four to ten years old.

Ohio

"The Bumbly Pool" is a show of music, stories, and interviews for family listening which airs on Thursdays from 11:00 a.m. to 11:30 a.m. on WRUW, 91.9 FM, Cleveland, Ohio.

Oklahoma

"Kids Radio Show" has been awarded "best in the state" for the past five years. An educational "sitcom musical adventure" aimed at family audiences, it's aired on Saturdays from 11:00 a.m. to 11:50 a.m. on KSPI, 93.7 FM, Stillwater, Oklahoma.

Oregon

"Skinnamarink," a program of stories and music, is aired Saturdays from 10:00 a.m. to 11:00 a.m. and Tuesdays from 4:00 p.m. to 5:00 p.m. on KMUN, 91.9 FM, Astoria, Oregon.

Pennsylvania

"Kid's Corner," WXPN, 88.9 FM, Philadelphia, is an award-winning show hosted by Kathy O'Connell, co-host of the now defunct "Kids America" (see page 202); it airs weekdays from 7:00 p.m. to 8:00 p.m. Kathy works music and stories around two half-hour themes. Targeting listeners from six to twelve, she asks questions which kids answer by calling in. Kids also perform once a week during the "On Stage" segment.

"Cinekyd Radio Playhouse," WRDV, 89.3 FM, Warminster, Pennsylvania, is a weekly half-hour program created by seven- through eighteen-year-olds at Cinekyd Enterprises, Inc. A nonprofit organization, Cinekyd enables kids to experiment with all aspects of the broadcast media. Using sound effects, characterization, and suspenseful plots, productions recall old-time radio shows and can appeal to listeners of all ages.

Vermont

"Just Kidding" has been produced and hosted for more than ten years by Jon Gailmor, who invites early-elementary-age children to be the stars as they share their songs, stories, and opinions with family audiences. Broadcast on WDEV, 550 AM, Waterbury, it airs on Saturdays from 8:05 a.m. to 8:30 a.m.

"Children's Radio Hour," targeted to family audiences, offers music, stories, and interviews with kids. Aired Monday through Thursday from 3:30 p.m. to 4:30 p.m., it can be heard on WGDR 91.9 FM, Goddard College, Plainfield.

Virginia

"Pooh Corner" is a program of music and stories for children ages four through eight. Broadcast Sunday mornings at 9:00 on WVRU, 89.9 FM, Radford, "Pooh Corner" is produced and prerecorded by students of Radford University. It has been airing since September 1985.

Washington

"The Round Table" is a ninety-minute program of stories and music targeting listeners age six to adult, aired live on Saturday mornings at 10:00 on KAOS 89.3 FM, Olympia. Elana Freeland is the producer.

"C-Trends," KNHC, 89.5 FM, Seattle, is a weekly half-hour program designed for and by teenagers. In a magazine format, the program offers interviews, sports, commentary, new music, and more. Teenagers are involved in the broadcasting as well as in the writing and editing.

Washington, D.C.

"Radio Road Gang" is produced by Pamela Brooke, who also produced "Songs Jumping in My Mouth," a series of thirteen half-hour programs on NPR around 1984.

Radio Road Gang
P.O. Box 90482
Washington, D.C. 20090-0482
(202) 544-2791

"Child's Play" is a live show of music, stories, and interviews for seven-to twelve-year-olds, aired Saturday mornings from 8:00 to 9:00 on WPFW, 89.3 FM. Children serve as interviewers, hosts, and production assistants. "Child's Play" is produced by Michael Hagbourne.

"Pass It On," also produced by Michael Hagbourne, is a one-hour program of interviews and panel discussions revolving around teenage issues. Airing Fridays at 6 p.m. on WPFW, it targets an audience of thirteen-to-nineteen-year-olds.

"Children's Radio Theatre" was a series of dramatized stories produced in Washington, D.C. Nationally distributed until late 1987, this superb material is not being aired presently. For home use, "Cabbage Soup" and "Beauty and the Beast" can be purchased on cassette from A Gentle Wind in Albany, New York (see page 53).

Wisconsin

"Dancing Dog Radio," hosted by performer Willie Sterba, is targeted to children from six to twelve years old. In English and Spanish, it features vocabulary building and live and recorded music. It can be heard on WYMS, 88.9 FM, Tuesdays and Thursdays from 6:00 p.m. to 6:30 p.m. Milwaukee Public Schools Radio, which airs this show, offers a variety of programs for children, so contact them for their monthly program guide. Write to WYMS, Drawer 10K, 5225 West Vilet Street, Milwaukee, Wisconsin 53201.

"Secret Clubhouse," WYMS, 88.9 FM, Milwaukee, is a call-in show geared to five-through twelve-year-olds. On the air since 1985, this half-hour show can be heard Mondays, Wednesdays, and Fridays at 6:00 p.m.

With stories geared for children ages five to ten, "Fairy Tales" is aired Tuesdays and Thursdays from 6:00 p.m. to 6:30 p.m. on WYMS, 88.9 FM, Milwaukee. Joan Schmidt produces this prerecorded show.

Bibliography

Allison, Christine. *I'll Tell You a Story, I'll Sing You a Song*. New York: Delacorte Press, 1987.

Arnold, Arnold. *Your Child's Play*. New York: Simon and Schuster, 1955.

Cass-Beggs, Barbara. *Your Baby Needs Music*. New York: St. Martin's Press, 1978.

Choksy, Lois; Robert Abramson, Avon Gillespie, and David Woods. *Teaching Music in the Twentieth Century*. Englewood Cliffs, N.J.: Prentice-Hall, Inc., 1986.

Duke, C. R. "Integrating Reading, Writing, and Thinking Skills into the Music Class." *Journal of Reading* (Newark, Delaware), November 1987.

Elkind, David. *The Hurried Child*. Reading, Mass.: Addison-Wesley, 1981.

Gesell, Arnold, M.D., and Frances L. Ilg, M.D. *Infant and Child in the Culture of Today*. New York: Harper and Row, 1943.

Glazer, Tom. *Tom Glazer's Treasury of Songs for Children*. New York: Grosset and Dunlap, 1964.

Gordon, Edwin T. *The Psychology of Music Teaching*. Englewood Cliffs, N.J.: Prentice-Hall, 1972.

Halpern, Steven, with Louis Savary. *Sound Health*. New York: Harper and Row, 1985.

Healy, Jane. *Your Child's Growing Mind*. New York: Doubleday, 1989.

Holt, John. *How Children Learn*. Revised edition. New York: Delacorte Press/Seymour Lawrence, 1983.

Hood, Phil, ed. *Artists of American Folk Music*. Quill/A Guitar Player and Frets Book. New York: William Morrow, 1986.

McDonald, Dorothy T. *Music in Our Lives: The Early Years.* Washington, D.C.: National Association for the Education of Young Children, 1979.

Merrion, Margaret Dee, and Marilyn Curt Vincent. *A Primer on Music for Non-Musician Educators.* Bloomington, Ind.: Phi Delta Kappa Educational Foundation, 1988.

"Music Enrichment Produces Giftedness." Article about a report by Emily P. Cary describing research findings in the *Roeper Review. Gifted Child Monthly,* July/August 1987.

Rivera, A. Ramon, and Thelma Gruenbaum. *To: Music and Chidren with Love!!* Brookline, Mass: exPressAll, 1979.

Seeger, Ruth Crawford. *Animal Folk Songs for Children.* Garden City, N.Y.: Doubleday, 1950.

Taubman, Hyman Howard. *How to Bring Up Your Child to Enjoy Music.* Garden City, N.Y.: Hanover House, 1958.

Trelease, Jim. *The New Read-Aloud Handbook.* New York: Penguin Books, 1989.

Wilson, Frank R., M.D. "Music and Your Child." Brochure. St. Louis, Mo.: MMB Music Inc., 1988.

Winn, Marie. *The Plug-In Drug.* New York: Penguin Books, 1985.

Wohlstadter, Ellen. "Music and the Young Child." *Child Care Center,* November 1986.

Artist Index

For indexes to the *All Ears* Sampler of Music arranged according to age appropriateness and topic, see pages 62–66.